Sight-Sing a New Song

A Workbook for
Music Reading Basics

JENNIFER
KERR BREEDLOVE

WORLD LIBRARY PUBLICATIONS

Sight-Sing a New Song

© 2005, World Library Publications
the music and liturgy division of J. S. Paluch Company, Inc.
3708 River Road, Suite 400, Franklin Park, IL 60131-2158.

ISBN 1-58459-236-2

All rights reserved under United States copyright law.
No part of this book may be reproduced or transmitted in any form or by any means, mechanical,
photographic, or electronic, including taping, recording, photocopying, or any information storage
or retrieval system, without the written permission of the copyright owner.
Printed in the United States of America.

Project Editor: Alan J. Hommerding
Assistant Editor: Marcia T. Lucey
Cover Design: Christine Enault
Book Layout/Design: Kathy Ade
Music Engraving: Steve Fiskum

WLP Customer Care: 800 566-6150
Toll-free Fax: 888 957-3291
wlpcs@jspaluch.com
www.wlpmusic.com

TABLE OF CONTENTS

PRELUDE: *Jennifer Kerr Breedlove*

How to Use *Sight-Sing a New Song*

UNIT ONE: *page 1*

Rhythmic Studies: **Pulse and Meter (Simple and Compound)**

Melodic Studies: **Whole Steps and Half Steps; the Major Scale; Intervals**

UNIT TWO: *page 15*

Rhythmic Studies: **Note and Rest Values in Simple Meter**

Melodic Studies: **The Musical Alphabet on the Keyboard and Grand Staff**

UNIT THREE: *page 29*

Rhythmic Studies: **Reading Rhythm Patterns in Simple Meter**

UNIT FOUR: *page 37*

Melodic Studies: **Major Scales on the Grand Staff; Key Signatures; Accidentals**

Melodic & Rhythmic Studies: **Reading Melodies in Various Keys, in Simple Meter**

UNIT FIVE: *page 53*

Rhythmic Studies: **Note and Rest Values in Compound Meter**

Melodic & Rhythmic Studies: **Reading Melodies in C, G, F, and D Major, in Simple Meter**

UNIT SIX: *page 67*

Rhythmic Studies: **Common Time and Cut Time**

Melodic Studies: **Minor Scales and Key Signatures**

Melodic & Rhythmic Studies: **Reading Melodies and Rhythms in Simple and Compound Meter, in Minor Keys**

UNIT SEVEN: *page 85*

Rhythmic Studies: **Finishing Touches — Pickups and Triplets**

Melodic & Rhythmic Studies: **Reading Melodies and Rhythms in Simple and Compound Meter, in Major and Minor Keys**

UNIT EIGHT: *page 91*

Musical Miscellany: **Articulation, Dynamics, Tempos, and Following the Road Map**

APPENDIX A (The Major Scales and Their Key Signatures) *page 105*

APPENDIX B (The Natural Minor Scales and Their Key Signatures) *page 109*

APPENDIX C (The Bass Clef and Treble Clef Staff, The Piano Keyboard) *page 113*

Prelude

There are countless singers in the world, many of them in church choirs and other music ensembles, who forever belittle their own musical ability because they "can't read music." They see the myriad little black dots on the page as some grand mystery decipherable only by experts, far beyond their reach. (Even though those of us who do read music stand in awe of their ability to hold so many notes in their aural memories, a feat that would utterly confound us if we were to try it!) Sadly, the only reason most of them cannot "read" is because no one ever gave them the tools to learn, or someone tried to teach them in the same way one would teach an instrumentalist to read music.

Most basic music reading seems to be geared toward learning to play an instrument. Expecting such a method to work for a singer is unrealistic and counterproductive, because of the very different needs of the two disciplines. Think of it: If you want to play a "C" on the piano, you simply locate and strike the correct key, and you hear the note. The same is true for almost any other instrument. Reading music becomes a simple process of decoding the symbols that enable you to depress the correct valve or key at the right time, to produce the correct sound.

Singers have no such valves, keys, frets, or other hardware to tell us if what we're singing is correct or not. In order to produce the correct pitch at the correct time, we have to *know in our minds what the music is supposed to sound like before we make a sound*. This is a radically different way to conceive of music when contrasted with the instrumental approach. For us, learning to read music is not so much deciphering a straightforward symbol system as it is learning to read and write a rich new language we've seen and heard all around us for years, but never had the tools to translate.

Fortunately, for most of us this process engages us with a language we already "speak" to some degree, one we can hear fluently and to which we respond instinctively. Music is something that has been a part of our lives since we were children, and in the same way children learn their own mother tongue, we have picked up the language of song by listening to it and "speaking" it over the years. Like children learning to read books, the process of translating the written notation of this language is a skill we will spend years developing and honing. So we are still essentially "learning" a language we already know.

This book is intended to give volunteer church musicians the basic tools they need to learn the fundamentals of sight-reading music, from a singer's perspective. Obviously, as with any tools, learning to use and apply them will be possible only with time and practice. Although this book was initially developed for use in a class setting, I hope that students working through it will continue to practice and review, working and reworking their way through the different concepts, applying them to their own singing and music-making, while gaining confidence and proficiency over time.

Good luck! Learning to read music need not be an intimidating or insurmountable task; take your time, be patient with yourself (and others!), and enjoy your new-found talent!

Jennifer Kerr Breedlove

How to Use
Sight-Sing a New Song

This workbook is designed for use by both instructors and learners, so that all are literally "on the same page" while working through the various units.

Instructors: To teach from this workbook, you will need a piano or other keyboard instrument to play some of the lesson materials and musical examples, and a chalkboard or whiteboard to illustrate some of the examples. If you have a board with pre-drawn music staff lines on it, so much the better!

Depending on the amount of time you are allotted for each session, the entire workbook can be covered in an eight-week time frame, though the material covered in the eight units will not be of equal difficulty or of equal importance. Do not hesitate to do part of a unit in one class; just make sure that single topics are covered in a comprehensive manner.

If you are using this method for members of your own choir who do not read music, or whose music-reading skills are somewhat limited, you may wish to supplement the exercises and examples with pieces that you are learning in choir rehearsals.

Learners: The only thing you will need to use this workbook—aside from your eagerness to learn to read and sight-sing music—is a sharp pencil! There are exercises throughout the book, and your written answers go right in the book so you can refer to them in the future. As you progress through the workbook, make helpful notes for yourself that you can go back to time and time again as you continue to use and gain confidence with these skills.

There are three appendices in the back of the book, including a "keyboard" for you. Most of the answers to the written exercises can be checked against one of these three appendices.

Throughout this book, frequent comparisons are made between learning to read and sight-sing music and learning to read and speak a language. Some of the work we do when we learn to read and speak a language can be done alone, but it is best done and better retained when we do it in "conversation" with others. You may want to find a "sight-singing buddy" to work with in your class sessions and perhaps one other time during the week. This will speed up and strengthen your progress!

UNIT ONE

Rhythmic Studies:
Pulse and Meter (Simple and Compound)

Melodic Studies:
Whole Steps and Half Steps; the Major Scale; Intervals

RHYTHMIC STUDIES: *Pulse and Meter*

Rhythm in music is basically the division of time into organized, repetitive, and predictable segments, and the relationship of those segments to each other. It is ultimately much more basic than melody and more crucial that it be understood and grasped.

The basic unit in rhythm is the "pulse" or "beat." In essence, it is the division of time into equal repeating parts. The parts can be any size or length, but they must be equal. The easiest analogy is our own human pulse. When it is solid and steady, it indicates that we are healthy and functioning. When it is uneven, it implies ill health. When it is not present at all . . . well, that's usually not good.

So, imagine a steady **pulse** (no, this isn't official musical notation, but use your imagination!).

| | | | | | | | | | | | | | | | |

The next level of division of time is called **meter,**
the division of a pulse into a pattern of strong and weak beats.

| | | | | | | | | | | | | | | | |

When writing music, we refer to one of these statements of a meter pattern as a **measure** or **bar**. In this example, the section above would contain four measures.

REMEMBER: Rhythm in music, even at its most complicated, will almost always break down into patterns, or building blocks, of either two or three. How the building blocks are arranged will change, but the actual content of the blocks—two or three—will almost never change.

ORGANIZING THE BEATS: *Duple and triple meter*

In dividing the pulses into meter patterns, we can create either a **triple meter** (three beats per measure)

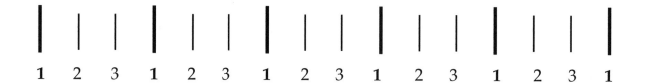

or a **duple meter** (two or four beats per measure)

or

DIVIDING THE BEATS: *Simple and compound meter*

A further level of division can occur between the beats (pulses) themselves. Take for example, a piece in duple meter, with four beats per measure:

If we divide each beat into two equal parts, we have a **simple meter**:

(count) **ONE** and TWO and THREE and FOUR and **ONE**

(think) *Mon* - day, *Tues* - day, *Wednes* - day, *Thurs* - day

If we divide each beat into three equal parts, we have a **compound meter**:

(count) **ONE** and – a TWO and – a THREE and – a FOUR and – a **ONE**

(think) *El* – e – phant, *Por* – cu – pine, *El* – e – phant, *Por* – cu – pine

It's often difficult, or even impossible at times, to tell the difference between simple and duple meter, or compound and triple meter, by ear alone. The key is to find the strong beats. In a later lesson we'll learn how to tell one from the other in printed music.

UNIT ONE, Page 3

One more time, with feeling:

- When we say a piece is in either duple or triple meter, we are talking about the way the beats are grouped together. Almost every piece of music is going to be one or the other.
- When we say a piece is in either simple or compound meter, we are talking about the way the beats are divided within each one. Almost every piece of music is going to be one or the other.
- "Is it duple or triple?" and "Is it simple or compound?" are two distinct questions we must ask of every piece of music we sing.
- Thus we are dealing with four possible combinations: simple duple, simple triple, compound duple, compound triple (see examples below).

EXAMPLES:

For each example, the instructor will set the beat (or pulse). Listen to each example at least two separate times:

1. The first time, listen for where the strong beats fall: beat ONE two, ONE two, ONE two. If this works and feels comfortable, it's probably in simple meter. If not, try beating ONE two three, ONE two three, ONE two three. If this feels more comfortable, it's probably in triple meter.
2. The second time, go within the beats: try counting ONE-and-two-and-three-and. If this is comfortable, it's probably simple meter. If not, try ONE-and-a two-and-a three-and-a. If this feels better, it's probably compound meter.

Simple duple meter: "Joy to the World"

Simple triple meter: "Amazing Grace"

Compound duple meter: "What Child Is This"

Compound triple meter: "Jesu, Joy of Man's Desiring" (the organ part)

Note: At this stage, and really throughout this book, do *not* skip steps in any of the processes and try to leap to the conclusion! The seemingly endless little steps we take are crucial to our understanding of the music. Even the most seasoned professionals seldom skip steps in sight-reading music; they simply have become so accustomed to taking all the myriad little steps and processes that they can go through them very quickly.

AURAL EXERCISES

a. **Clapping rhythms** in duple and triple meter (clap after instructor).

b. **Identifying duple and triple meter:** With your instructor's help, identify the meter of some familiar hymns or songs by locating the pattern of the strong beats.

c. **Identifying compound and simple meter:** With your instructor's help, identify the meter of different pieces of music by listening for two or three divisions within the beats.

RHYTHMIC STUDIES: *Vocabulary*

Bar (colloq.): Same as measure

Bar line: The vertical line indicating the end of one measure and the beginning of another

Beat: Same as pulse.

Compound meter: Each beat divides into three equal parts ("*El*-e-phant, *Por*-cu-pine, *El*-e-phant, *Por*-cu-pine").

Duple meter: A meter with two or four beats per measure

Measure: One statement of a meter pattern

Meter: Division of beat into regular pattern of strong and weak

Metronome: A tool, mechanical or electronic, that emits a steady pulse at a prescribed number of beats per minute. An invaluable aid for practicing rhythm exercises!

Pulse: Divides time into equal parts. Examples: your pulse, the second hand on a watch, etc.

Simple meter: Each beat divides into two equal parts ("*Mon*-day, *Tues*-day, *Wednes*-day, *Thurs*-day").

Triple meter: A meter with three beats per measure

MELODIC STUDIES: *Whole Steps and Half Steps*

The half step is the smallest distance between pitches used in Western music. It is easy to find on a piano keyboard. Any white key and the black key closest to it are a half step apart

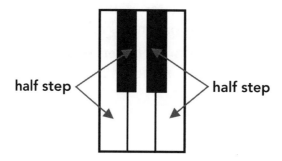

as are any two white keys that do not have a black key between them.

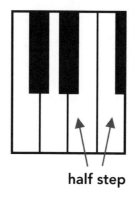

(Think of the theme from *Jaws*.)

The whole step is equal to two half steps. It is also easy to find on a piano keyboard. Any two white keys that have a black key between them are a whole step apart.

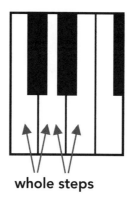

(Think of the first few notes of "Mary Had a Little Lamb.")

All of our music can be broken down into patterns of whole steps and half steps. With the rhythmic divisions we learned in the previous lesson, these are the most basic building blocks of our study.

THE MAJOR SCALE

The major scale consists of a pattern of eight pitches, in a pattern of whole and half steps, that forms the basis for most Western musical forms.

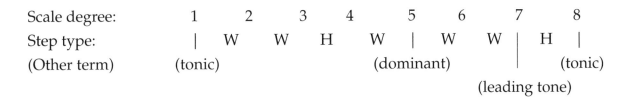

A **scale** is a pattern of eight pitches encompassing one **octave**, using a specific pattern of whole steps and half steps.

There are literally countless possible combinations one could come up with, and probably at least a dozen have been used with some regularity over the last few centuries in Western music. Most of the music we sing in our parishes is based on only two: the **major** scale and the **minor** scale. (We will deal with the minor scale in Unit Six).

When we say a scale is major or minor, we are referring to its **quality**. The quality of the scale we are studying in this unit is major.

 ## VOCAL EXERCISE

Sing the major scale several times, starting on different notes, calling the first note "One" and counting upward. When you get to 7, say "Sev" (just for ease in singing) and instead of 8, sing "One" again (we'll explain why later).

```
                          1—1
                    7-          -7
                 6-                -6
              5-                      -5
           4-                            -4
        3-                                  -3
     2-                                        -2
  1-                                              -1
```

Learning to Use the Amazing Sound System Hardwired into the Human Brain!

Is there anyone reading this who has not had the thoroughly annoying experience of waking at 3 a.m. with some phrase from a song or a tune running through their head over and over and over again? What many people do not realize is that this very ability is one of our greatest assets, and can be channeled into an invaluable tool for us as musicians and readers. We have, built into our brains, a highly sophisticated record-and-playback system whose limitations are set only by our mental discipline and willingness to work and harness it.

Just as an exercise, sing our major scale again, the way we did previously:

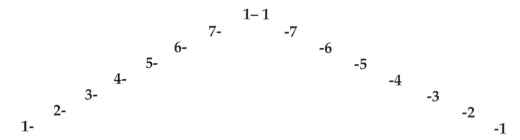

Now, without making any sound, hear yourself sing the scale once again, this time in your head. Try to reproduce as accurately as possible inside your head what it sounded like when you sang it out loud.

Next, without actually singing it aloud, hear yourself sing the scale again, only starting on a different note. (If you need to sing the starting note out loud to get yourself started, do that; but let your mind, rather than your voice, do most of the work.)

"Hear" yourself sing the scale several times, varying the speed, volume, and even style of your vocal sound. Try "hearing" your favorite pop singer or opera star sing it. Be creative!

When this is comfortable for you, keep practicing this skill with different songs or hymns, simply training your brain to be able, at will, to "hear" music inside itself without needing to involve your physical ears.

This is a skill employed constantly by professional musicians and those who sight-read music on a daily basis. In reality, much of the "sight-reading" professional singers do is more accurately a second reading of music they have already "sung" in their heads, often in fast-forward mode, so that there are no real surprises the first time they sing the music out loud. Some are even skilled enough that they can mentally review upcoming measures while their physical voices are singing a few bars behind.

As you work through the exercises in this book, practice this form of "silent singing" *consistently* and *consciously*. Try to hear exercises in your head before you sing them aloud, unit by unit. For many students, it is this very discipline that makes the connection between the theoretical knowledge offered in this book and the ability to apply it to actual singing situations.

MELODIC STUDIES: *Scale Degree and Function*

NOTE: *The basic method we'll be using in this unit and throughout the course is the same concept Maria uses with the von Trapp children in* The Sound of Music. *Watch the "Doe, a deer" scene a few times!*

Once the basic sequence of whole and half steps in a major scale is comfortable and fluent (and for most of us who grew up singing hymns in church, it is and has been since we were children, whether we knew it or not), the different notes within a major scale will exert their own influence and develop a particular "sound" in our ears. Think of the involuntary way we feel compelled to complete the phrase's final two notes when someone plays or sings the cliché "shave and a haircut" sequence. Our ears will not let the unfinished phrase just sit there; we need to resolve it.

We assign each note in the scale a number, called its **scale degree.** This refers to the number assigned to any given pitch within a scale, in relation to the first note of the scale. The starting note of any scale is called the **first degree**, the second note is the second degree, the third note is the third degree, etc.

Usually we will refer to each scale degree simply by its number. However, there are a few degrees, which are more important and serve specific functions, that also have names.

Tonic is another name for the first degree of a scale, the "home" pitch toward which most melodies are oriented. Most melodies will start and/or finish on the "tonic" note of their scale. It is also sometimes called the **keynote**.

Leading tone is another name for the seventh degree of a scale, because it will almost always "lead" back to the tonic. A good example is the familiar song "America." Sing the first phrase: "My country, 'tis of thee, sweet land of liberty, of thee I . . ." We can hardly stop on this note; we *have* to go on to the final "sing!" The word "I" falls on the leading tone of the scale and pulls us back up to the tonic (on the word "sing").

Dominant is another name for the fifth degree of a scale. After the tonic, this degree is the most structurally important, or "dominant," in the scale. Like the leading tone (but not as emphatically), it will usually lead us back to the tonic.

VOCAL EXERCISE

Sing the following patterns to familiarize yourself with the feel of the tonic, dominant, and leading tone pitches of a scale:

Tonic and dominant (degrees #1 and #5, ascending)

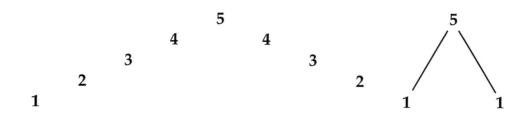

Tonic and dominant (degrees #1 and #5, descending)

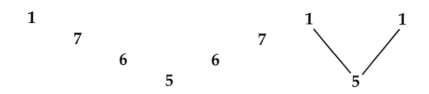

Tonic and leading tone (degrees # 1 and #7)

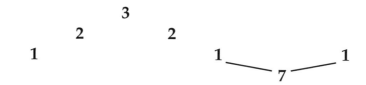

MELODIC STUDIES: *Intervals*

 Memorize this concept:

• An **interval** is the distance between two notes in a scale, including the notes themselves.

For example, the first degree and the third degree are at an *interval of a third*. The first degree and the sixth degree are at an *interval of a sixth*. The second degree and the fifth degree are at an *interval of a fourth*. The first degree and the eighth degree are at an *interval of an octave* (thus they will sound as the same note, only higher or lower).

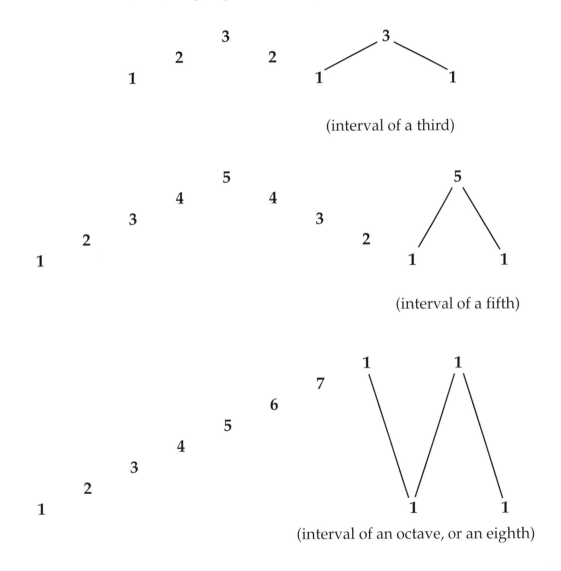

EXERCISES

Identifying whole steps and half steps visually

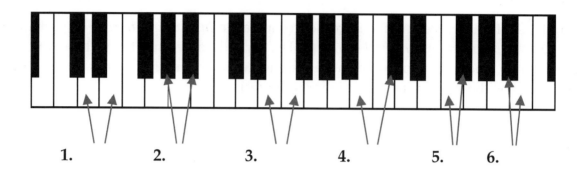

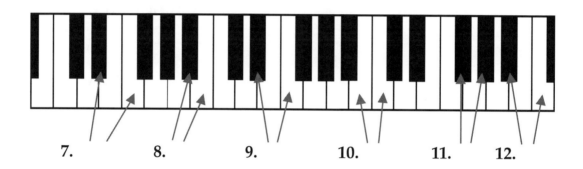

Identifying whole steps and half steps aurally

For each of the following, you will hear two pitches, either a half step or a whole step apart. Identify, using "ws" or "hs" to indicate which you think it is.

1.   2.   3.   4.   5.   6.

Singing melodic patterns using degree numbers

Sing each of the following:

a. 1 – 2 – 3 – 1 – 2 – 3 – 4 – 5 – 1 – 5 – 1
b. 1 – 2 – 3 – 4 – 5 – 4 – 5 – 1 – 2 – 3 – 4 – 3 – 4 – 2 – 3 – 4 – 5 – 4 – 3 – 2 – 1
c. 1 – 2 – 3 – 4 – 5 – 3 – 1
d. 1 – 2 – 3 – 4 – 5 – 3 – 4 – 2 – 5 – 3 – 4 – 2 – 3 – 2 – 1
e. 1 – 2 – 3 – 1 – 3 – 4 – 5 – 1 – 3 – 5 – 3 – 1
f. 1 – 3 – 5 – 6 – 5 – 3 – 4 – 2 – 1 – 5 – 6 – 5 – 1
g. 1 – 3 – 5 – 6 – 5 – 6 – ↑7 – ↑1 – 7 – 5 – 6 – 4 – 5 – 3 – 4 – 2 – 1 – ↓7 – ↓6 – 7 – 1

(Note that in exercise g. we were using some scale degrees in the upper and lower octaves.)

Singing intervals using degree numbers

Note that the numbers in bold are skips that you sang previously by step.

Seconds: 1 – 2 – 1 ,
          2 – 3 – 2 ,
          3 – 4 – 3, etc.

Thirds: 1 – 2 – 3 – 2 – **1 – 3 – 1 – 3 – 1**
          2 – 3 – 4 – 3 – **2 – 4 – 2 – 4 – 2**
          3 – 4 – 5 – 4 – **3 – 5 – 3 – 5 – 3**, etc.

Fourths: 1 – 2 – 3 – 4 – 3 – 2 – **1 – 4 – 1 – 4 – 1**
          2 – 3 – 4 – 5 – 4 – 3 – **2 – 5 – 2 – 5 – 2**
          3 – 4 – 5 – 6 – 5 – 4 – **3 – 6 – 3 – 6 – 3**, etc.

If you're having trouble negotiating a jump when attempting to sing intervals or melodies, just try using the exercise on page 8. (Sing all pitches *between* your starting pitch and the one you want in order to get it into your head.) Then try jumping directly to it.

Example:
To sing: 1 – 3 – 4 – 2 – 1
Think: 1-2-3 – 4-3-2 – 1

UNIT ONE, Page 13

MELODIC STUDIES: *Vocabulary*

Dominant: Another name for the fifth degree of a scale. After the tonic, this degree is the most structurally important, or "dominant," in the scale. Like the leading tone (but not as emphatically), it will usually lead us back to the tonic.

Half step: The smallest distance between pitches used in Western music. Can easily be found on a piano keyboard: any white key and the black key closest to it, or any two white keys that do not have a black key between them, are a half step apart (the distance between the third and fourth degree of a major scale). Think of the theme from *Jaws*.

Interval: The distance between two notes in a scale, including the notes themselves. For example, the first degree and the third degree are at an *interval of a third*. The first degree and the sixth degree are at an *interval of a sixth*. The second degree and the fifth degree are at an *interval of a fourth*. The first degree and the eighth degree are at an *interval of an octave* (thus they will sound as the same note, only higher or lower).

Keynote: Another name for the first degree of a scale, the note from which the scale takes its "key" (Unit Two).

Leading tone: Another name for the seventh degree of a scale, so called because it will almost always "lead" back to the tonic. Think of the first phrase of "America": "My country, 'tis of thee, sweet land of liberty, of thee I *sing*."

Octave: If the vibration of a pitch is cut in half, it will sound as the same pitch, only higher. If the vibration of a pitch is doubled, it will sound as the same pitch, only lower. We call the difference between these pitches one *octave*. The major and minor scales contain eight notes, or degrees (*oct* means "eight").

Scale: A pattern of eight pitches encompassing one *octave*, using a pattern of whole steps and half steps.

Scale degree: The number assigned to any given pitch within a scale, in relation to the first note of the scale. The starting note of any scale is called the first degree, the second note is the second degree, the third note is the third degree, etc.

Scale quality: The particular pattern of whole and half steps in a scale. Scale quality types include major, minor, and chromatic. The quality of the scale we are studying in this unit is major.

Tonic: Another name for the first degree of a scale, the "home" pitch toward which most melodies are oriented. Most melodies start and/or finish on the tonic note of their scale.

Whole step: Equal to two half steps. Can easily be found on a piano keyboard: any two white keys that have a black key between them are a whole step apart (the distance between the first and second degree of a major scale). Think of the first few notes of "Mary Had a Little Lamb."

UNIT TWO

Rhythmic Studies:
Note and Rest Values in Simple Meter

Melodic Studies:
The Musical Alphabet on Keyboard and Grand Staff

RHYTHMIC STUDIES: *Note and Rest Values*

Note Values:

Whole note	𝅝
Half note	𝅗𝅥
Quarter note	♩
Eighth note	♪
Sixteenth note	𝅘𝅥𝅯

These note shapes indicate the length of a note. They do not indicate the number of beats, only the relative length of the note. The number of beats is determined by the time signature, which we will study later in this unit.

1 whole note 𝅝 = 𝅗𝅥 𝅗𝅥 2 half notes

2 half notes 𝅗𝅥 𝅗𝅥 = ♩ ♩ ♩ ♩ 4 quarter notes

4 quarter notes ♩ ♩ ♩ ♩ = ♪♪♪♪♪♪♪♪ 8 eighth notes

8 eighth notes ♪♪♪♪♪♪♪♪ = 𝅘𝅥𝅯𝅘𝅥𝅯𝅘𝅥𝅯𝅘𝅥𝅯𝅘𝅥𝅯𝅘𝅥𝅯𝅘𝅥𝅯𝅘𝅥𝅯𝅘𝅥𝅯𝅘𝅥𝅯𝅘𝅥𝅯𝅘𝅥𝅯𝅘𝅥𝅯𝅘𝅥𝅯𝅘𝅥𝅯𝅘𝅥𝅯

16 sixteenth notes

> Sometimes eighth notes and notes of smaller value are grouped together with horizontal lines called "beams." These mean the same thing as the individual "flags" on single eighth notes; they simply help the eye group the notes together more easily.

EXERCISES

"Musical Math"

Of course, the divisions aren't usually as cut-and-dried as the example above. Using the same principles as basic math and fractions, we can make countless combinations of note values that would fit into the same time space:

Try a few more on your own:

𝅗𝅥 =   =   =

𝅗𝅥 =   =   =

𝅗𝅥 =   =   =

o =   =   =

o =   =   =

o =   =   =

UNIT TWO, Page 16

RESTS

A rest is a specified length of silence in music. Rests are valued and counted like notes.

Rest Values   Whole rest

Half rest

Quarter rest

Eighth rest

1 whole rest   =   2 half rests

2 half rests   =   4 quarter rests

4 quarter rests   =   8 eighth rests

More "Musical Math"

Now try a few of the same exercises as above, but try mixing notes and rests:

𝅗𝅥 = ♩ 𝄽 = ♩ ♪ 𝄾 = 𝄾 𝄾 ♪ 𝄾 ♫

Try a few more:

𝅗𝅥 =   =   =

𝅗𝅥 =   =   =

𝅗𝅥 =   =   =

𝅝 =   =   =

𝅝 =   =   =

𝅝 =   =   =

TIME SIGNATURES: *Simple Meter*

The time signature consists of two vertically placed numbers at the beginning of a piece of music. The top number tells how many beats are in each measure, and the bottom number tells what kind of note receives one beat. Frequently used time signatures in simple meter are:

    4   means four beats per measure
    4   means a quarter note (♩) receives one beat

Example:

    3   means three beats per measure
    4   means a quarter note (♩) receives one beat

Example:

    2   means two beats per measure
    4   means a quarter note (♩) receives one beat

Example:

    2   means three beats per measure
    2   means a half note (♩) receives one beat

Example:

EXERCISES: *Rhythm and Time Signature*

1. Clap the rhythmic patterns your instructor claps first for you.

2. Identify time signatures:

    4 ____ beats per measure

    4 ____ gets one beat

    3 ____ beats per measure

    2 ____ gets one beat

    5 ____ beats per measure

    4 ____ gets one beat

    2 ____ beats per measure

    2 ____ gets one beat

Write time signatures for the following:

    1.   **4** beats per measure; a half note (𝅗𝅥) gets one beat

    2.   **3** beats per measure; a quarter note (♩) gets one beat

    3.   **2** beats per measure; a half note (𝅗𝅥) gets one beat

    4.   **3** beats per measure; an eighth note (♪) gets one beat

MELODIC STUDIES: *Musical Alphabet*

The musical alphabet is made up of seven letter names: A, B, C, D, E, F, G. Each of these letters names a specific note or pitch. Every eight notes, or octave, the alphabet begins with A again. These letters also correspond to the names of the white keys on a piano keyboard.

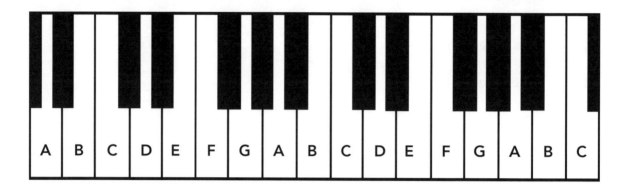

You can use the groupings of two or three black keys to help you find your pitches. C is always to the left of the two black keys together; B is always to the right of the three black keys together; F is always to the left of the three black keys together.

The notes on the keyboard are arranged so that if you start on C, you can play a major scale (with the correct pattern of whole steps and half steps) on white keys only.

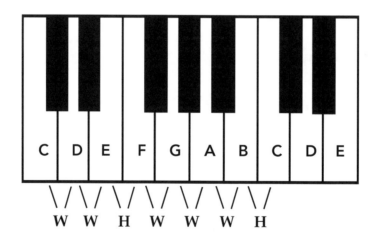

UNIT TWO, Page 20

The black keys are described in relation to their neighboring white keys. They can be *sharp*, a half step higher (written as ♯), or *flat*, a half step lower (written as ♭). Notice that each black key can have more than one name, depending on which note it relates to.
For example, F♯ and G♭ are the same pitch. The technical term for this is **enharmonic**.

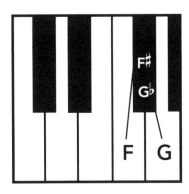

Also notice that when there is no neighboring black key, the nearest white key can be referred to as sharp or flat. C can also be referred to as B♯; E can also be referred to as F♭.

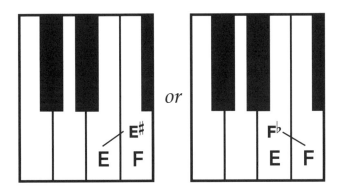

Using sharps and flats and our pattern of whole steps and half steps, we can describe exact pitches for major scales starting on any note. Use your keyboard drawing in Appendix C to figure half and whole steps.

Major scale pattern:	(1) - W - W - H - W - W - W - H
C major	C - D - E - F - G - A - B - C
G major	G - A - B - C - D - E - F♯ - G
F major	F - G - A - B♭ - C - D - E - F

! Note that in every scale the letters are named consecutively. For example, in F major, we describe the fourth degree as B♭, not A♯, so as not to skip a letter name.

Correct:

D major   D - E - F♯ - G - A - B - C♯ - D

Incorrect:

D major   D - E - G♭ - G - A - B - D♭ - D

MELODIC STUDIES: *The Grand Staff*

The staff is made up of five lines and four spaces and is the basis for musical notation. When two staffs are connected, as above, they are referred to as the **grand staff**. The **grand staff** encompasses pitches from very low to very high and is used primarily for keyboard (or choral) music.

Music, like printed words, is read from left to right. At the beginning of any staff you will always see a **clef**. This symbol indicates what pitches will be found on any line or space in the staff for a given piece of music. The most common clefs, and the ones with which we will be working, are:

Treble clef (or G clef)   Bass clef (or F clef)

The treble clef encompasses higher pitches, and the bass clef encompasses lower pitches. Generally, in a modern choir, sopranos and altos sing using the treble clef, and basses sing using the bass clef. Tenors must be conversant with both; sometimes they sing from the bass clef, and sometimes they sing from the treble clef but one octave lower.

NOTES ON THE GRAND STAFF: *Treble and Bass Clef*

NOTE: Up until now, most of our work has been fairly logical and intuitive. The section we're now moving into will have less to do with logic and more with simple rote memorization. Admittedly, this is one of the least interesting ways for most people to learn, but in the case of locating pitches on the staff, it's by far the best way. Mnemonics, little memory-aid tricks, are provided for each one to speed the process along, but practice and repetition are really the only route to success here. Ten or fifteen minutes a day spent with any hymnal or piece of music, just identifying pitches, will bring you great results.

All notes on the staff can be identified as "line notes" or "space notes."
The space notes are as follows:

Mnemonics (from low to high):   **Bass clef: All Cows Eat Grass**
                                  Treble clef: **F A C E**

Memorize these!

The line notes are as follows:

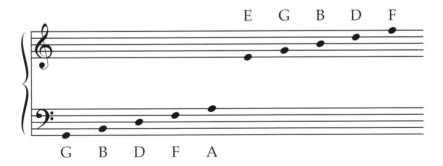

Mnemonics: Bass clef: **G**ood **B**oys **D**o **F**ine **A**lways
                Treble clef: **E**very **G**ood **B**oy **D**oes **F**ine

Similar, aren't they? **Memorize them anyway!**

Another important reference point to grasp early on is the location of middle C.

Think of the grand staff as a set of eleven lines, of which C is the middle (eleventh) line.

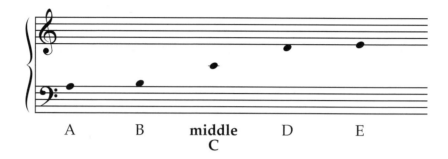

Now we separate them, but we still place C between the treble staff and the bass staff. It can be notated either above the bass staff or below the treble staff; it's the exact same note:

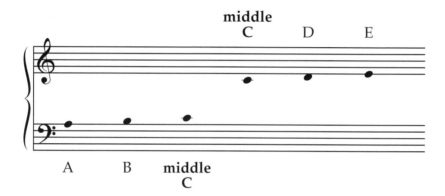

Middle C is a line note, but not on any of the existing staff lines. When we want to place a note on a line not already part of the staff, we simply add it for that one note. This is called a **ledger line** (see next page for further explanation).

Therefore, middle C is notated on the first ledger line above the staff in the bass clef, and on the first ledger line below the staff in the treble clef.

LEDGER LINES

As we have seen, sometimes we want to sing a note that does not fit neatly onto the staff. Fortunately, we have **ledger lines** to assist us. These enable us to add a line or two (or more) to a staff as needed, for a single note at a time. Very rarely, a bass section will be asked to sing down below the staff, past A, G, and F, all the way down to an E or even a D.

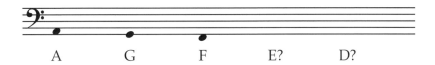

You'll notice we run out of staff lines once we get to F, so we'll just add a ledger line where we'd like the E and D to go.

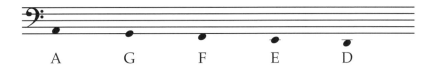

Likewise, a soprano part occasionally goes up to an A or B, for which we can add ledger lines for the extra notes.

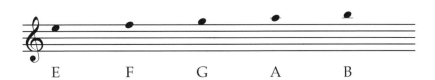

The same principles can apply to tenor and alto parts as well. Sometimes the alto will descend to notes low enough that we would normally write them in the bass clef:

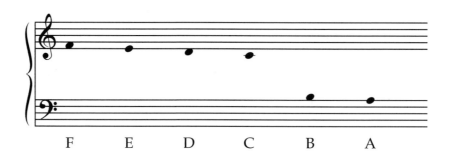

F   E   D   C   B   A

Obviously, writing alto or tenor parts on a full grand staff whenever they moved into one another's territory would be difficult to read and take up too much space, so we simply use ledger lines to accomplish the same thing.

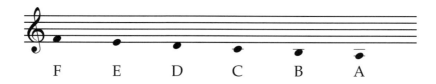

F   E   D   C   B   A

Although the examples above are about as high or low as you will ever need to go as singers, remember that there is theoretically no limit to how high ledger lines can take you.
Flute players frequently travel up into stratospheric territory:

! Remember that the five-line staff is an arbitrary thing—it developed over time as music changed and developed. Ledger lines enable us to enlarge it as much as we need at any given moment. Obviously your mnemonic devices won't work here. Until you become comfortable reading the ledger-line notes you frequently encounter in your own voice part, you may simply need to count up or down the appropriate number of lines until you can name the note you want.

UNIT TWO, Page 26

EXERCISES: *Pitch Identification and Notation*

Identify the following treble clef pitches.

Identify the following bass clef pitches.

Notate the following pitches in treble clef. (For most of the notes there will be more than one correct answer; try to notate different versions of the same pitch name.)

F   G   C   B   E   D   A   E   C   D   E   B   A   F   E   C

G   E   F   E   F   D   C   A   C   B   G   B   A   D   C   F

UNIT TWO, Page 27

Notate the following pitches in the bass clef.

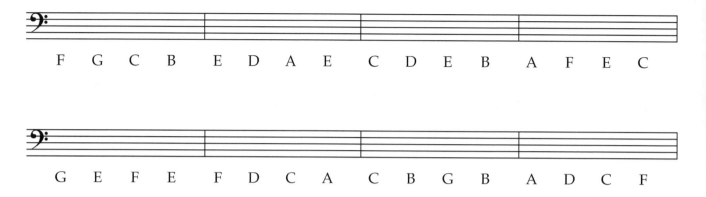

> **For more practice** in this skill, use any printed music (such as a hymnal) to continue to identify pitches. Before long, you will find yourself using mnenomics less and less often, identifying pitches instantly! The more practice you get, the easier it will become.
>
> The sooner you can simply identify the pitches without resorting to counting lines and spaces or using mnemonics, the sooner sight reading will become fun rather than brain-draining.

Rhythmic Studies:
Reading Rhythmic Patterns in Simple Meter

UNIT THREE

RHYTHMIC STUDIES: *Reading Rhythmic Patterns in Simple Meter*

COUNTING RHYTHMS

The time signature is the basic foundation from which we read rhythmic patterns. The time signature anchors us in the structure of the music and makes it much easier to find our place again if we get lost or confused. Remaining aware of the time signature in our mental background keeps us aware of exactly where in the measure we are.

The first step in setting up this "background" is deciding which of several possible choices will be most helpful with a given piece of music. We do this by looking at the piece as a whole and identifying the smallest note value that occurs within the time signature.

BEAT NOTES: *Counting beat number*

Occasionally, the smallest note in a hymn or song will simply be the beat itself. In 4/4 time, if the smallest note is a quarter note, then all we need to do is count the beat number itself, and our background counting scheme will be:

In 3/4 time:

UNIT THREE, Page 29

In $4/2$ time:

BEATS DIVIDED IN HALF: *Count "one – and"*

If the smallest note or rest value that occurs is one-half the "beat note" value (for example, eighth notes in $4/4$ or $3/4$ time, quarter notes in $4/2$ or $3/2$ time, or sixteenth notes in $4/8$ time), then we have to add a syllable in between the beats:

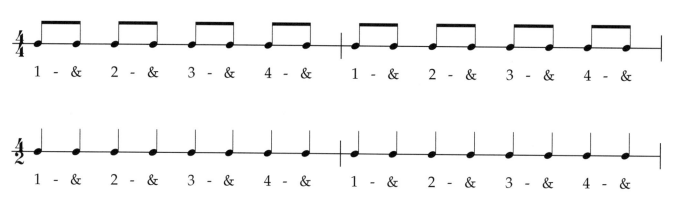

BEATS DIVIDED INTO FOUR: *Count "one–ee–and–a"*

If the smallest note or rest value that occurs is one-fourth the "beat note" value (for example, sixteenth notes in $4/4$ or $3/4$ time, or eighth notes in $4/2$ or $3/2$ time), then we need yet more syllables to articulate all of the rhythms between the beats clearly. So we say:

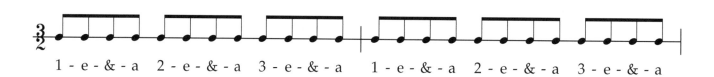

UNIT THREE, Page 30

Applying these syllables to actual rhythmic patterns:

Of course, we seldom get only neat quarters, eighths, or sixteenths in a given piece of music, so we need to learn how to apply these counting patterns to more complicated rhythms.

COUNTING RHYTHMS: *With beat numbers*

We note that for the time signature:

  4 means four beats per measure

  4 means a quarter note (♩) receives one beat

Therefore our basic counting pattern will be:

  One, two, three, four. One, two three, four.

Since there are no note values smaller than the quarter-note beat, we don't need to worry about anything smaller.

Going back to the example: The first half note gets two beats in **4/4** time, so under the first half note we count:

Then, each of the following quarter notes gets one beat, and one count:

We continue through the example, starting with "1" at the beginning of each new bar.

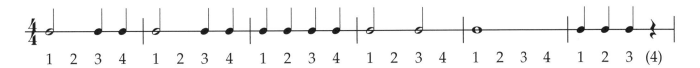

UNIT THREE, Page 31

Clapping the rhythmic patterns

Once you have written in the beats under the rhythms the next step is to sing or clap the pattern. Eventually you will be able to skip this step and not always write the beats in, but don't rush it. Remember what we said in Unit One about not skipping steps.

First, set up your basic beat pattern, counting out loud:

One, two, three, four. One, two three, four.

Then, clap the pattern over your counting (refer to aural example).

> Like finding the tonic or keynote in a scale or piece of music, finding the "one" or downbeat of the measure will always orient us rhythmically.
>
> If you get lost reading a rhythmic pattern, just keep the pulse going and wait for the next "one" beat to jump back in.

 EXERCISES *(Each one is started for you.)*

1. Quarter note gets the beat; speak: One two three, one two three, one two three…

2. Half note gets the beat; speak: One two three four, one two three four

3. Eighth note gets the beat; speak: One two three four, one two three four

COUNTING RHYTHMS: *With half beats*

Here is an example of a pattern that requires a different background count:

If a quarter note gets one beat, then the presence of eighth notes means we need to consider notes that are half a beat in length. So this time, the counting pattern we set up will be:

One-and two-and three-and four-and. One-and two-and three-and four-and

As with the previous example, we assign the correct counts to each of the note values in the example:

As we can see, in this pattern a quarter note gets a full beat, with number plus "and;" an eighth note gets just one spoken "syllable." We complete the process:

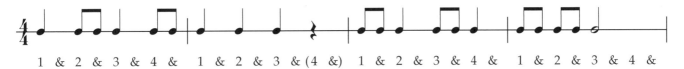

EXERCISES

Write the beats under the following patterns, then count out loud, in rhythm.

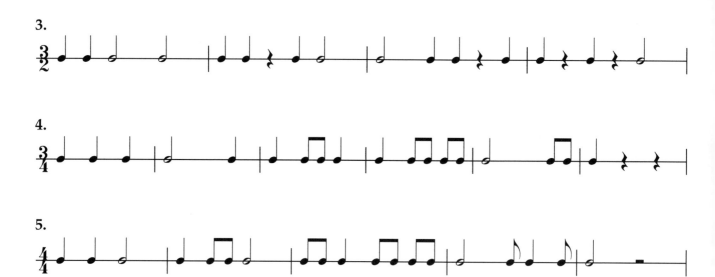

COUNTING RHYTHMS: *With quarter beats*

Next let's divide the beat even further:

Here, we need a way to keep track of all the little beat subdivisions that will account for the sixteenth notes. So we count:

1-e-&-a 2-e-&-a 3-e-&-a   1-e-&-a 2-e-&-a 3-e-&-a   1-e-&-a 2-e-&-a 3-e-&-a   1-e-&-a 2-e-&-a 3-e-&-a

A quarter note, still taking up an entire beat, will receive the full "one-ee-and-a."

1-e-&-a

The eighth is only half as long and gets only two syllables, and the sixteenth gets the smallest amount of time the counting pattern will allow:

1-e-&-a 2-e-&-a 3-e-&-a   1-e-&-a 2-e-&-a 3-e-&-a   1-e-&-a 2-e-&-a 3-e-&-a   1-e-&-a 2-e-&-a 3-e-&-a

 **EXERCISES**

Write the beats under the following patterns, then count out loud, in rhythm.

1.

2.

3.

4.

5.

THE DOT

When we see a dot to the right of a note (or rest), it means that the dotted value is increased by one-half the note's (or rest's) value.

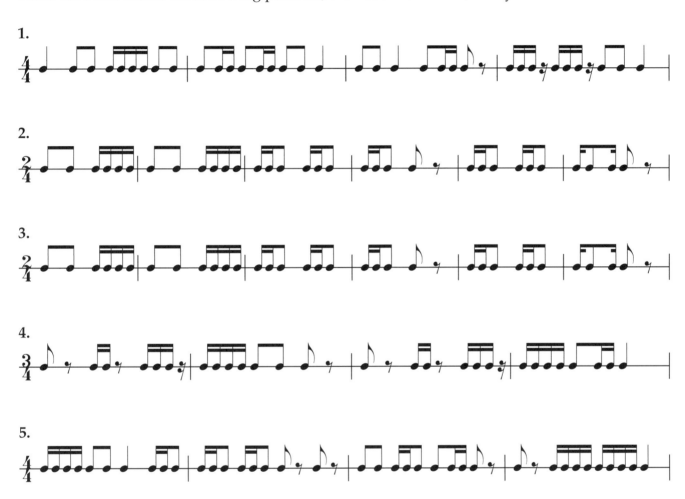

UNIT THREE, Page 35

EXERCISES

For each of the following,

1. Decide which counting pattern you will use by figuring out whether the smallest note value in each exercise is the beat itself, half the length of a beat, or one quarter the length of the beat.

2. When you have decided on your counting pattern, write it in beneath the appropriate note values for each exercise below, as we did in previous exercises.

3. Counting the background pattern verbally, clap each rhythmic pattern.

UNIT THREE, Page 36

UNIT FOUR

Melodic Studies:
Major Scales on the Grand Staff; Key Signatures; Accidentals

Melodic and Rhythmic Studies:
Reading Melodies in Various Major Keys in Simple Meters

MAJOR SCALES: *On the Grand Staff*

In Unit One, we learned that all major scales consist of a pattern of eight pitches, in a specific pattern of whole and half steps:

Scale degree:	1	2	3	4	5	6	7	8
Step type:	| W	W	H	W	| W	W	| H	|
(Other term)	(tonic)				(dominant)		(leading tone)	(tonic)

We also learned that the notes on the keyboard are arranged so that if we start on C, we can play a major scale (with the correct pattern of whole steps and half steps) on white keys only.

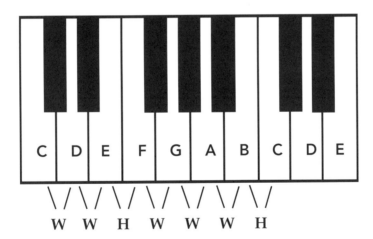

Our next step will be to learn to build major scales, using this pattern of whole and half steps, starting on any pitch in the musical alphabet.

Using the notation we've learned, as well as your sample keyboard, add sharps (♯) and flats (♭) as appropriate to the following scales so that they fit the pattern of whole steps and half steps on the major scale. (G major is done for you here; correct notation for these exercises can be found in Appendix A at the end of the book.)

G major

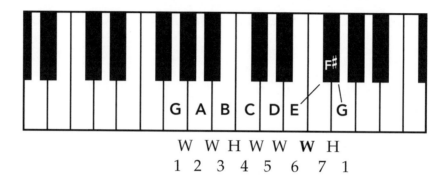

Note that from scale degree 6 to 7, in order to create a whole step, we must raise the F to an F♯. Therefore, we'd notate a G major scale on the staff as follows:

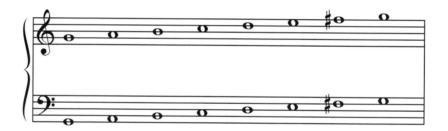

F major

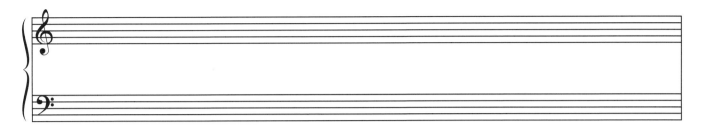

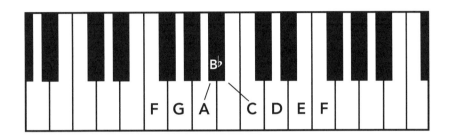

D major

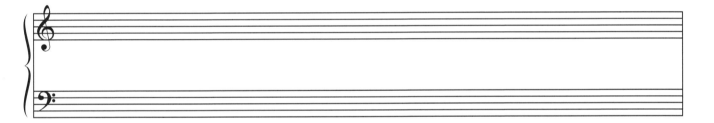

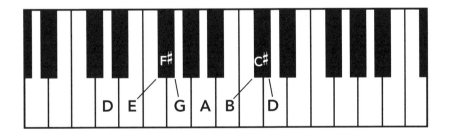

A major

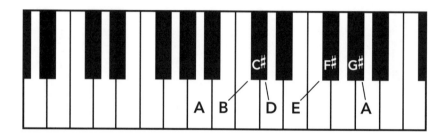

When notating a major scale, or any sequence of notes moving by adjacent scale degrees (sometimes expressed as "stepwise" motion), they are noted line-space-line-space-line or space-line-space-line-space. Notes that jump line-line-line or space-space-space are "skipping" notes.

We will observe this in more detail later.

KEY SIGNATURE

In every major scale, the same pitches will always be sharp or flat to make the pattern of whole and half steps fit correctly. G major will *always* have an F♯; D major will always have an F♯ and C♯; F major will always have a B♭.

To avoid having to write out every sharp and flat, and to make identification of the key easier, we use a **key signature**. Glance through some printed music at random; for most of it you will probably see, immediately to the right of the clef, one or more sharps or flats. This indicates that throughout the piece, or unless otherwise indicated, those particular sharps and flats will always be observed. The key signature will also tell us what key a piece of music is written in, and thus which note is assigned scale degree one.

EXAMPLE:

G major scale:

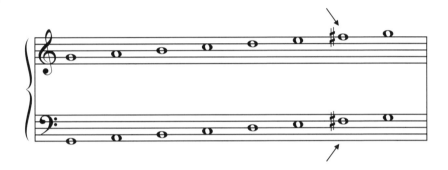

Notice that the G major scale contains one sharp, F♯. Therefore we can notate F♯ at the beginning of a piece and know that the notated pitch F throughout will be played or sung as F♯, and that the keynote of the piece is G:

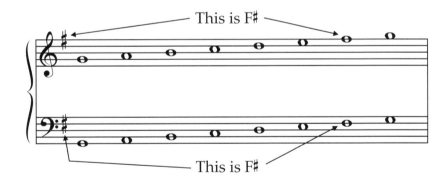

Since C major contains no sharps or flats, if you see no key signature you can usually assume that the piece is in the key of C major.

(For further examples, refer to Appendix A, containing all twelve major scales and key signatures.)

> The best way to learn key signatures and pitch notation is simply to memorize! You could figure it out every time, but that's very time-consuming and even frustrating. If you can become immediately familiar with key signatures containing up to three sharps or three flats, you will be in very good shape.

MEMORY AIDS: *Sharp Keys*

Key signatures that use sharps: G major, D major, A major, E major, B major, F♯ major, C♯ major

Order of sharps: F♯, C♯, G♯, D♯, A♯, E♯, B♯

Look at the last sharp in the key signature; the corresponding major key will be one letter name up from that. For example:

➤ The key signature is one sharp, F♯. One letter up from F♯ is G. The key is G major.

➤ The key signature is three sharps, F♯, C♯, and G♯. One letter up from G♯ is A. The key is A major.

MEMORY AIDS: *Flat Keys*

Key signatures that use flats: F major, B♭ major, E♭ major, A♭ major, D♭ major, G♭ major, C♭ major

Order of flats: B♭, E♭, A♭, D♭, G♭, C♭, F♭

Look at the second-to-last flat in the key signature; that will be the corresponding major key. For example:

➤ The key signature is two flats, B♭ and E♭. The key is B♭ major.

➤ The key signature is four flats, B♭, E♭, A♭, and D♭. The key is A♭ major.

An exception: If the key signature is one flat (B♭), the key is F major. You just have to memorize that one!

READING MELODIES: *On the Grand Staff*

Once we are familiar with the notation of pitches on the staff and the concepts of scale degrees and key signature, we can read the actual melodies on the staff using the following procedure:

1. Identify the key of the piece (key signature).
2. Identify the keynote, or first scale degree.
3. Assign scale degree numbers to the notated pitches. Write numbers beneath each pitch.
4. Sing the melody using scale degree numbers as we did in Unit One.

Using the melody above, we'll go through four steps to sing it.

1. Look at the key signature. We see one sharp, F♯. We know (because we've either memorized it or looked it up) that F♯ is the signature key of G major.

2. Using our knowledge of pitch notation (because we've either memorized it or are using our handy little mnemonics), we know that in the treble clef G is notated on the second line of the treble staff. In the bass clef, G is notated either on the first (or bottom) line or on the fourth (or top) space of the bass staff. We identify and mark as scale degree 1 all the G's we can find in this melody.

3. We then assign scale degree numbers to the remaining pitches. Remember that when a line note goes to the next space note (as with the first two pitches), it is moving to the next scale degree in either direction. When a line note goes to the next line note or a space note to the next space note, the scale degree number skips one note, and so on.

If you have trouble with interval jumping, use the exercise from Unit One to make the jump from scale degree 3 to scale degree 6:

Sing 3 (-4-5-) 6, 3 – 6 back and forth a few times until you can make the jump.

Don't get hung up on the visuals and printed music here. Once you have written in the scale degrees, trust your mind and your ears.

4. Once we have assigned scale degree numbers and are given the starting pitch, we can now sing the entire melody.

Recognize this melody? It's the first phrase of the hymn tune ST. THOMAS, usually sung with the words "Tantum Ergo."

THE NATURAL

Now that we have learned the sharp (♯) and the flat (♭), we need to learn one more pitch symbol—the **natural**.

This symbol stands simply for any note that is neither sharp nor flat. We use it most often in relation to another new term—the **accidental**.

ACCIDENTALS

Occasionally we will want to use a note that is not within a piece's particular key signature. In order to specify those notes, we simply indicate a sharp, a flat, or a natural next to the specific note:

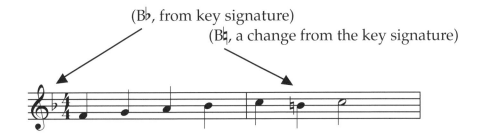

! Note that any accidental added to a note is good for the remainder of that measure, but not beyond. In this example, because the first B is indicated as a natural, the second (in the same measure) is natural, too.

But this one, in the next measure, automatically reverts to the B♭ of the key signature.

Sometimes the publisher will kindly give what are known as "courtesy accidentals," indicating in parentheses little reminders about what would normally be a given:

Both of the notes with parenthetical accidentals would still be B♮ and B♭ even without an accidental, but it is sometimes there anyway just to help us remember.

If we only wanted one B♮ and desired the second B in the second measure to revert to the key signature, we'd have to indicate it specifically:

(This is, of course, a B♭ again.)

Reading melodies with accidentals on the grand staff

When reading a melody with accidentals, we need to employ an additional step.

1. Identify the key of the piece (key signature).
2. Identify the keynote, or first scale degree.
3. Assign scale degree numbers to the notated pitches. Write numbers beneath each pitch.
4. New step: Check melody for any accidentals. Decide whether the accidental will raise or lower the pitch you would normally expect to sing. Indicate which by an arrow pointing either up or down.
5. Sing the melody using scale degree numbers as we did in Unit One.

Let's try one, working through the steps again but including the new process of checking for accidentals:

1. Look at the key signature. We see one flat, B♭. We know that the B♭ is the signature of the key of F major.

2. We know that F is notated on the first space of the treble staff, so we identify and mark as scale degree 1 all the F's we can find.

3. We assign scale degree numbers to the remaining pitches.

4. Now we check for accidentals and find two: The B♭ of the key signature is cancelled out by a natural in the second measure, raising the pitch a half step; and the G in the third measure becomes a G♯, raising that pitch a half step as well. So we indicate with arrows how to treat each accidental.

5. Once we have assigned scale degree numbers, noted where the accidentals fall, and are given the starting pitch, we can now sing the entire melody.

EXERCISES: *Reading Melodies on the Staff*

Read these melodies in major keys, following the five steps we just learned.

8.

9.

MELODIC STUDIES: *Vocabulary*

Accidental: The sign (♯, ♭, ♮) placed before a note that indicates the raising or lowering of its pitch

Clef (treble or bass): Symbol at the beginning of the staff indicating where notated pitches are to be sounded

Flat (♭): Lowers pitch of a note by a half step

Grand staff: Treble staff and bass staff connected to encompass pitches from very low to very high; used primarily for keyboard writing

Key signature: A pattern of sharps or flats indicating which pitches will be observed as sharp or flat throughout the entire piece of music; notated immediately to the right of the clef on the staff. The key signature also tells us where to find the keynote, or first scale degree, of the piece.

Ledger line: A line added above or below the staff to notate a pitch that is higher or lower than the five lines of the staff

Line note: A note written on a line on the staff

Middle C: The pitch that lies between the treble and bass staffs; notated on the first ledger line above the staff in the bass clef, and on the first ledger line below the staff in the treble cleff

Natural (♮): 1. A note that is neither sharp or flat (Don't B♯, don't B♭, just B♮!); 2. as an accidental, cancels out a sharp or flat that has occurred earlier

Sharp (♯): Raises pitch of a note by a half step

Space note: A note written between two lines on a staff

Staff: Five horizontal lines on which music is notated

MELODIC AND RHYTHMIC STUDIES:

Reading Melodies in Various Keys in Simple Meter: Putting It All Together

> Our previous exercises have separated melodic and rhythmic elements for ease in learning. Now we will begin to combine the two. There's nothing new here; you're just putting together what you already know!

First, after identifying the time signature, read the rhythm of the melody, first clapping against the best "background pattern" you can decide on, and then speaking on the syllable *ta*.

Second, using the steps established in Unit Four, pages 43 and 44, practice reading the following melodies by scale degree number only.

Third (and only after accomplishing the first two!), read the melody in scale degree numbers in the correct rhythm, or if it is easier, on the syllable *ta*.

UNIT FIVE

Rhythmic Studies:
Note and Rest Values in Compound Meter

Melodic and Rhythmic Studies:
Reading Melodies in C, G, F, and D major, in Simple Meter

RHYTHMIC STUDIES: *Note and Rest Values in Compound Meter*

We remember from Unit One our definitions of simple meter and compound meter:

Simple meter: Each beat divides into two equal parts.
   (***Mon*** - day, ***Tues*** - day, ***Wednes*** - day, ***Thurs*** - day)

Compound meter: Each beat divides into three equal parts.
   (***El*** – e – phant, ***Por*** – cu – pine, ***El*** – e – phant, ***Por*** – cu – pine)

We have worked in simple meter in the previous units; now we will learn to apply the same note values and note types to compound meter.

THE TIE

When we wish to create a note that stretches over a bar line or creates some sort of notational difficulty, we **tie** two notes together with a curved line above or beneath them. They will sound as a single note whose length is the sum of their two values.

♩	sounds exactly like	♪‿♪
♩.	sounds exactly like	♩‿♪ or ♪‿♪‿♪
𝅗𝅥	sounds exactly like	♩‿♩ or ♩.‿♪

⟹ *But be careful; the tie looks a lot like . . .*

UNIT FIVE, Page 53

THE SLUR

A slur is also a curved line that connects two notes above or below, but with this difference: A slur affects the *way* a series of notes will be played or sung, not how long any of them will be counted. When two or more notes are slurred together, they are played or sung in a smooth, connected manner.

A tie will always connect two notes of the same pitch. A slur will join two or more notes of different pitches.

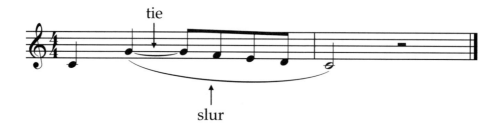

Smaller Note Values

In the previous unit, we learned about whole notes, half notes, quarter notes, eighth notes, and sixteenth notes. The note values can easily be divided further by adding additional flags or beams to them:

Sixteenth note

Thirty-second note

These values could be divided almost infinitely, but we seldom need to deal with any value smaller than a thirty-second note.

Smaller valued rests similarly add a flag to the existing rest:

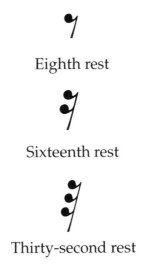

Eighth rest

Sixteenth rest

Thirty-second rest

TIME SIGNATURES: *In Compound Meter*

As we know, the time signature consists of two vertically placed numbers at the beginning of a piece of music. The top number indicates how many beats are in each measure, and the bottom number indicates what kind of note receives one beat. In the case of compound meter, however, the division of each beat into three equal parts calls for a different manner of interpretation.

Time signatures frequently used in compound meter are:

6	9	12	6
8	8	8	4

! **Clue:** If the top number is larger than 3 and divisible by 3, the piece is probably in compound meter.

Figuring time signatures in compound meter is done differently from simple meter.

By our previously established system, the following would be true:

6   means there are six beats per measure
8   means an eighth note (♪) gets one beat

CALCULATING TIME SIGNATURES: *In Compound Meter*

We know that in compound meter each beat is divided into three parts.

Divide the top number by 3 to determine the number of beats per measure.

6
8   (6 ÷ by 3 = 2 beats per measure)

Then multiply the value of the bottom note by 3 to determine what kind of note gets one beat.

6
8   (♪ + ♪ + ♪ = ♩.)   Three eighth notes equal a dotted quarter, so therefore a dotted quarter note gets one beat.

Is this a little confusing? Perhaps. This explanation is for people who like to know why something works a particular way. It's just as easy simply to memorize the patterns!

Ideally, however, in compound meter we count the beat on a broader scale.

6 **8**	(2 beats per measure) (♩. gets one beat)	**9** **8**	(3 beats per measure) (♩. gets one beat)
12 **8**	(4 beats per measure) (♩. gets one beat)	**6** **4**	(2 beats per measure) (♩. gets one beat)

THE GOOD NEWS:

While this kind of counting will be very useful with music at faster tempos and as you become more skillful and comfortable with reading rhythms, in the beginning it will be much simpler to use the same basic method of counting we used in simple meter.

However, because of the division of beats into multiples of 3, we will need to break our habit of thinking of quarter notes as "a beat" (which, as we know, is only true in 4/4 or 3/4 and 2/4 time). In most compound meter music, the basic beat will be not the quarter (♩) or half (𝅗𝅥), but the dotted quarter (♩.) or dotted half (𝅗𝅥.)

And always remember as you count, that even if you're counting "one two three four five six" it should always have the feeling of two larger beats, with strong stress on "one" and "four": "ONE two three FOUR five six, ONE two three FOUR five six."

So let's look at our note relationships again, but for compound meter this time:

Note Relations in 6/8, 9/8 and 12/8

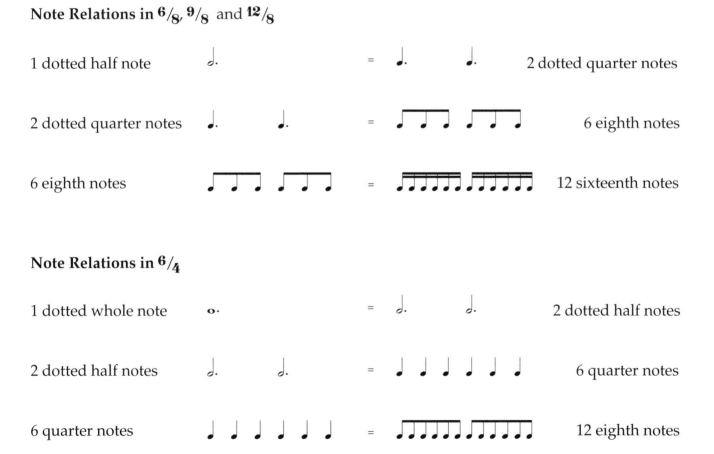

1 dotted half note	𝅗𝅥.	= 𝅗𝅥. 𝅗𝅥.	2 dotted quarter notes
2 dotted quarter notes	♩. ♩.	= ♫♫♫ ♫♫♫	6 eighth notes
6 eighth notes	♫♫♫ ♫♫♫	= ♬♬♬♬♬♬ ♬♬♬♬♬♬	12 sixteenth notes

Note Relations in 6/4

1 dotted whole note	𝅝.	= 𝅗𝅥. 𝅗𝅥.	2 dotted half notes
2 dotted half notes	𝅗𝅥. 𝅗𝅥.	= ♩ ♩ ♩ ♩ ♩ ♩	6 quarter notes
6 quarter notes	♩ ♩ ♩ ♩ ♩ ♩	= ♫♫♫♫♫♫ ♫♫♫♫♫♫	12 eighth notes

UNIT FIVE, Page 57

MUSICAL MATH: *In Compound Meter*

Remember our exercises in "musical math" from Unit Two?
They will look somewhat different in compound meter. Now, instead of dividing beats by 2, we are looking for 3 main subdivisions to the beat:

> **!** Note that in compound meter, one of the choices we do not want is:
>
> ♩. = ♩ ♩ ♩
>
> This not to say that we will never see this pattern in compound meter, but remember that in most compound meter patterns the quarter note is not the beat note.

Now try a few on your own. Notice that the examples given above contain many of the musical patterns common to compound meter. You can use many combinations of these in your own examples:

♩. ♩. =   =   =   =

♩. ♩. =   =   =   =

♩. ♩. =   =   =   =

♩. ♩. =   =   =   =

UNIT FIVE, Page 58

As we did with simple meter, let's also try a few that add rests into the pattern:

You'll notice as we continue (and perhaps you began to sense this in Unit Three), that as we play with the different rhythmic grouping of notes certain patterns recur.

In many ways it's like learning to read or write any new language. Think of how children learn to read. First they learn the individual letters and the sounds each letter makes, then they learn to put the letters together to sound out words. Eventually, as they do this more and more often, they no longer need to sound out words but simply recognize words they have read before. "Cat" no longer requires laboriously sounding out each letter; they simply see the word and recognize "cat."

It's the same with patterns of notes or rhythms. At this level we're still learning the "letters" and sounding out the "words." But be aware, as you continue to learn and practice, how over time some patterns will become more automatic and less intellectual. Just take your time and keep practicing!

COUNTING RHYTHMS

As with simple meter, we will count saying the actual beat numbers and adding syllables for the divided beats.

Compound Meter

As we said at the beginning of this unit, in the purest musical sense, a piece in **6/8** would be considered to have only two beats to the bar, with the dotted quarter (♩.) receiving one beat. For practical purposes, as long as the tempo stays moderate, it is usually easier just to count **6/8** or any other compound meter as though it had six beats to the bar, with the eighth note receiving one beat.

As before, we first look for the smallest note value and decide what background pattern we want to use to count.

"Beat" note:

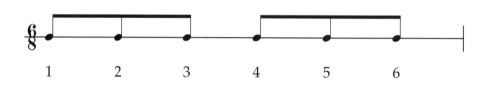

Beats divided in "half":

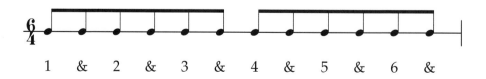

Let's look at some exercises:

When the smallest note is the "beat" note

In the example above, we see that the smallest note value is an eighth note. If we're counting as though there are six beats to the bar and an eighth note gets one beat, then we know we don't need to worry about anything smaller than the beat note. Our background pattern is simply, "One, two, three, four, five, six. One, two, three, four, five, six."

Therefore, each eighth note will get one count, quarter notes will get two counts, and dotted quarter notes will get three:

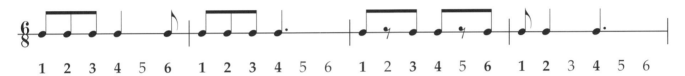

! A reminder: Even though we are counting in six, this pattern should still *feel* as though there are only two large beats per bar, as though you were counting "ONE-and-a TWO-and-a" rather than "ONE two three FOUR five six."

When the smallest note is the "half beat" note

In this exercise, if the smallest note is a sixteenth note, and we are counting nine eighth notes per measure, then we need to consider half beats. Therefore our background counting pattern here will be "One and two and three and four and five and six and seven and eight and nine and."

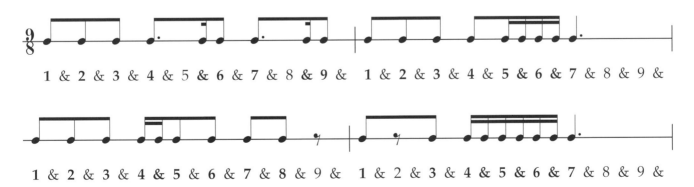

UNIT FIVE, Page 61

# EXERCISES

For the following rhythmic patterns in compound meter, do the following:
1. From the time signature, identify the number of beats per measure.
2. Decide which "background pattern" you need to use based on the smallest note value found in the exercise.
3. Assign numbers to each exercise within each background pattern.
4. Count the background pattern aloud while clapping each rhythmic pattern.

 **IMPORTANT:** When reading rhythmic exercises, be careful in choosing the best tempo (speed). Find the smallest note value in the exercise, and decide based on that value what tempo you will take. Otherwise you may find yourself at a faster tempo than the exercise will allow.

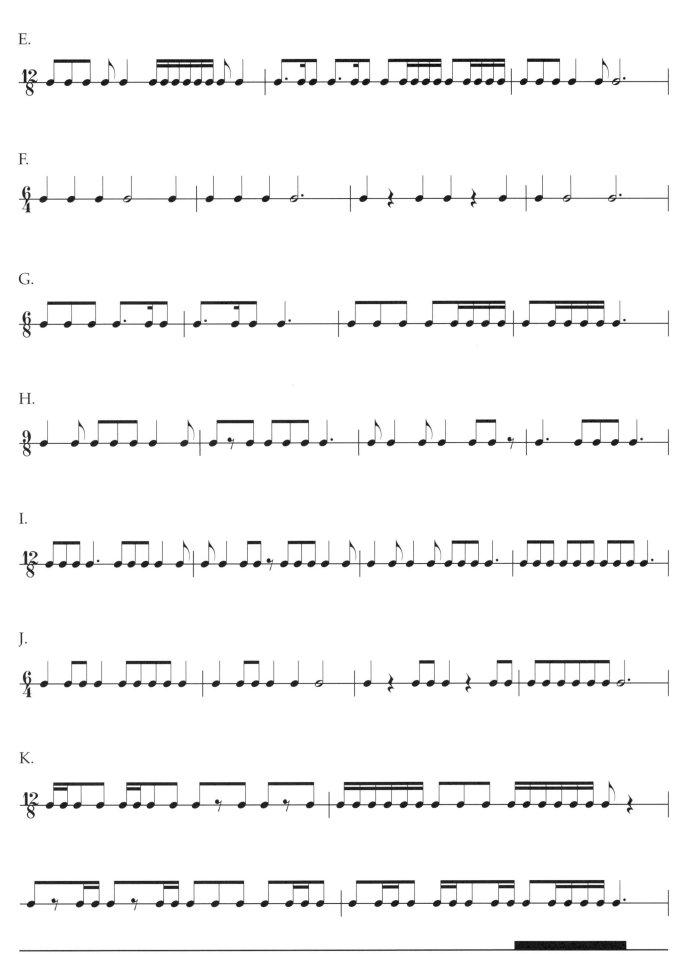

Reading melodies and rhythms in compound meter

Here are some melodies in compound meter to let you put together compound meter with reading rhythms. Again, there is nothing new here, just combining the things we've already learned.

First, after identifying the time signature, read the rhythm of the melody, first clapping against the best "background pattern" you can decide on, and then speaking on the syllable *ta*.

Second, using the steps established on Unit Four, page 43 and 44, practice reading the following melodies by scale degree number only.

Third (and *only* after accomplishing the first two), read the melody on scale degree numbers in the correct rhythm, or if it is easier, on the syllable *ta*.

A.

B.

C.

D.

E.

F.

UNIT FIVE, Page 65

UNIT SIX

Rhythmic Studies:
Common Time and Cut Time

Melodic Studies:
Minor Scales and Key Signatures

Melodic and Rhythmic Studies:
Reading Melodies and Rhythms in Simple and Compound Meter, in Minor Keys

COMMON TIME AND CUT TIME: 𝄴 *stands for "Common"*

If you peruse any hymnal or collection of music, you will very likely come to a piece with no apparent time signature, but simply a 𝄴 in the place where the time signature would normally go:

This is no great mystery. The 𝄴 merely stand for **common time**, the most common key signature: 4/4. Whenever you see the common time 𝄴 in the time signature, you know that the piece of music is in 4/4 time. It will have four beats in each bar, and a quarter note will get one beat.

You may also encounter a time signature much like the common time signature, only with a vertical line through the letter 𝄴:

As the notation suggests, this indicates "common time cut in half." Rather than 4/4 a piece with this time signature will be in 2/2 time, what we call **cut time**. It will be counted with two beats in each bar, with a half note getting one beat.

So just remember:

UNIT SIX, Page 67

MELODIC STUDIES: *Minor Scales and Key Signatures*

Our work so far has been based on the major scale pattern of whole and half steps. Varying patterns of whole and half steps can make different kinds of scales, but for our purposes we need only concern ourselves with the major and minor scales.

In the major scale the pattern of whole and half steps begins:

```
1    2    3    4    5
  W    W    H    W
```

In the minor scales the pattern changes by lowering the third degree by a half step. This changes the space between degrees 2 and 3 a half step and the space between degrees 3 and 4 a whole step:

```
1    2    3    4    5
  W    H    W    W
```

The element of the minor scale that is easiest to hear and identify is the lowered third degree, or the half step between scale degrees 2 and 3.

 EXERCISES

Listen while your instructor plays the first five notes of the C major scale. When it is played a second time, sing along using numerals for the scale degrees.

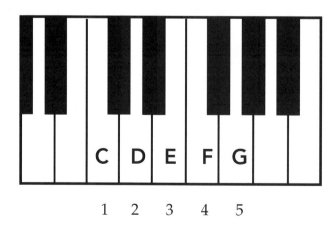

Now, listen while the third degree is lowered by a half step, changing the note E to E♭. Sing these first five degrees of a C minor scale:

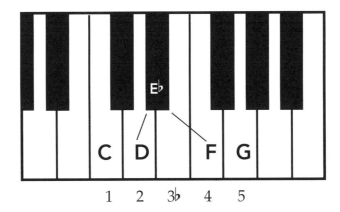

Repeat this exercise in several different keys until you are comfortable with the difference in the sound of major and minor.

 EXERCISE

Listen to each of the following patterns your instructor plays for you. Identify whether the quality of the pattern is major or minor.

1. 6.
2. 7.
3. 8.
4. 9.
5. 10.

THE MINOR SCALE

Recall that a scale is a pattern of pitches, spanning an octave, with a specific pattern of whole and half steps. It is this pattern of steps that determines the quality of the scale. Up until this point the scales we have worked with have had a major quality. Now we introduce the concept of the minor quality.

The pattern of whole steps and half steps in the natural minor scale is:

```
  1   2   3   4   5   6   7   1
    W   H   W   W   H   W   W
```

Look at the distance between scale degrees 7 and 1 (or 8). In the natural minor scale, this is a whole step. This means that the strong pull of the leading tone in the major scale will not occur here.

Different types of minor scales

Although in this book we will only be dealing with the most basic minor scales and keys, there are actually three types: natural minor, harmonic minor, and melodic minor. Each has a slightly different pattern of whole and half steps.

➤ NATURAL MINOR

The pattern of whole and half steps in the natural minor scale, the most common and the version we will be using in this book, is as follows (using the pitch names for C minor):

1	2	3	4	5	6	7	1
C	D	E♭	F	G	A♭	B♭	C
W	H	W	W	H	W	W	

Notice the whole step between scale degrees 7 and 1, rather than the strong half-step leading tone we are familiar with from the major scale.

➤ HARMONIC MINOR

Sometimes we still want that leading tone pull even in minor keys. For this we use the harmonic minor scale. It simply restores the leading tone to the existing natural minor scale:

1	2	3	4	5	6	7	1
C	D	E♭	F	G	A♭	B♮	C
W	H	W	W	H	W+H	H	

The large interval between scale degrees 6 and 7, called an **augmented second**, is the hallmark of the harmonic minor scale, and to our Western ears often injects a Gypsy, klezmer, or Middle Eastern flavor into the music.

➤ MELODIC MINOR

The melodic minor scale is more a theoretical construct than anything else; it exists to propose an alternative to the desired leading tone raised seventh degree without introducing the augmented second interval used in the harmonic minor scale. The melodic minor scale is different depending on whether one is ascending or descending.

Ascending, the melodic minor raises both the sixth and seventh scale degrees, thus reinstating the leading tone without the augmented second:

1	2	3	4	5	6	7	1
C	D	E♭	F	G	A♮	B♮	C
W	H	W	W	W	W	H	

Descending, the sixth and seventh degrees are lowered again, making it identical to the natural minor scale:

1	7	6	5	4	3	2	1
C	B♭	A♭	G	F	E♭	D	C
W	W	H	W	W	H	W	

EXERCISE: *Singing natural minor scales*

1. C major/C minor

After being given your starting pitch, sing a C major scale three times, first by step type (say, "one, whole, whole, half," etc.), then on scale degree numbers, then on pitch names:

C major:

Scale degree:	1		2		3		4		5		6		7		1
Step type:		W		W		H		W		W		W		H	
Pitch name:	C		D		E		F		G		A		**B**		**C**

Now sing a C minor scale:

C minor:

Scale degree:	1		2		3		4		5		6		7		1
Step type:		W		H		W		W		H		W		W	
Pitch name:	C		D		E♭		F		G		A♭		B♭		C

Repeat this exercise in several keys. You will need to write in the pitch names for each note before singing. Use the keyboard illustration in Appendix C for help.

2. G major/G minor

G major:

Scale Degree:	1		2		3		4		5		6		7		1
Step type:		W		W		H		W		W		W		H	
Pitch name:															

G minor:

Scale Degree:	1		2		3		4		5		6		7		1
Step type:		W		H		W		W		H		W		W	
Pitch name:															

3. F major/F minor

F major:

Scale degree:	1	2	3	4	5	6	7	1
Step type:		W	W	H	W	W	W	H
Pitch name:								

F minor:

Scale degree:	1	2	3	4	5	6	7	1
Step type:		W	H	W	W	H	W	W
Pitch name:								

4. D major/D minor

D major:

Scale degree:	1	2	3	4	5	6	7	1
Step type:		W	W	H	W	W	W	H
Pitch name:								

D minor:

Scale degree:	1	2	3	4	5	6	7	1
Step type:		W	H	W	W	H	W	W
Pitch name:								

5. E major/E minor

E major:

Scale degree:	1	2	3	4	5	6	7	1
Step type:		W	W	H	W	W	W	H
Pitch name:								

E minor:

Scale degree:	1	2	3	4	5	6	7	1
Step type:		W	H	W	W	H	W	W
Pitch name:								

Reminder: These patterns of whole and half steps are your good friends! You should have memorized the pattern for the major scale by now (if you haven't, do!) and now it will be useful to memorize the pattern for the minor scale as well. Memorization may not be the most interesting way to learn, to be sure, but it is often extremely useful.

MINOR KEY SIGNATURES: *Relative and Parallel Minor*

So far we have been resting comfortably in the belief that a key signature represents only one key, and have diligently memorized each signature and its attendant key. Now we learn that every key signature represents only one *major* key, and every major key has a corresponding *minor* key with the same key signature. Fortunately, it's not too difficult to distinguish between them.

Look at our keyboard and recall the C major scale:

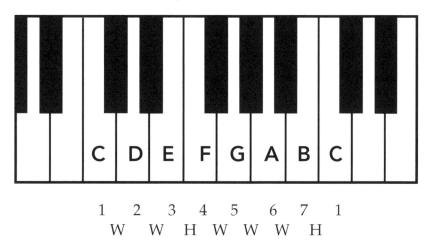

Now go down an interval of a third (to scale degree 6) and listen as your instructor plays an eight-note scale starting on A, on all white keys.

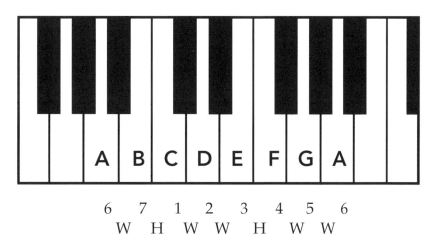

UNIT SIX, Page 73

When we check the pattern of whole and half steps this creates, we find that this is an A minor scale. Just as C is the major scale played with the correct pattern of whole and half steps without any black keys (sharps or flats), A is the *minor* scale played with the correct pattern of whole and half steps without any black keys (sharps or flats).

For every major key, there is a minor key that uses the same sharps or flats (in this case, none). We have just discovered that C major and A minor are such a pairing; we know that A minor has the same key signature as C major (no sharps or flats at all).

We say that A is the **relative minor** of C, and that C is the **relative major** of A.

In any major key, with any key signature, if we go down to scale degree 6 and play scale degree 6 - 7 - 1 - 2 - 3 - 4 - 5 - 6, we will hear a natural minor scale.

To find the relative major of a minor key, use the pattern of whole and half steps to locate scale degree 3. This will be the relative major of that minor key. The key signature of the relative major will also be the key signature of its relative minor.

> C major is relative to A minor
> G major is relative to E minor
> D major is relative to B minor
> F major is relative to D minor
> D major is relative to B minor
> E♭ major is relative to C minor

(For key signatures of all major and minor keys up to five sharps and flats, see Appendix B, Natural Minor Scales and Their Key Signatures.)

EXERCISES: *Singing relative major/minor scales*

Work through each key, first on scale degrees, then on pitch names.

After being given your starting pitch, sing a C major scale:

1	2	3	4	5	6	7	1
C	D	E	F	G	A	B	C

Now sing down the scale, but go all the way down to scale degree 6:

1	7	6	5	4	3	2	1	7	6
C	B	A	G	F	E	D	C	B	A

Now, starting on scale degree 6, sing up 8 notes:

6	7	1	2	3	4	5	6
A	B	C	D	E	F	G	A

This is the A minor scale.

For each exercise below, fill in the pitch names for each particular key.
First sing the exercise on scale degree numbers, and then on pitch names.

1. Sing an F major scale:

1	2	3	4	5	6	7	1
F	G	__	__	__	__	__	__

Now sing down the scale, but go all the way down to scale degree 6:

1	7	6	5	4	3	2	1	7	6
__	__	__	__	__	__	__	__	__	__

Now, starting on scale degree 6, sing up 8 notes:

6	7	1	2	3	4	5	6
__	__	__	__	__	__	__	__

This is the ___ minor scale.

UNIT SIX, Page 75

2. Sing a D major scale:

1	2	3	4	5	6	7	1
D	E	__	__	__	__	__	__

Now sing down the scale, but go all the way down to scale degree 6:

1   7   6   5   4   3   2   1   7   6

__ __ __ __ __ __ __ __ __ __

Now, starting on scale degree 6, sing up 8 notes:

6   7   1   2   3   4   5   6

__ __ __ __ __ __ __ __

This is the ____ minor scale.

3. Sing a B♭ major scale:

1	2	3	4	5	6	7	1
B♭	C	__	__	__	__	__	__

Now sing down the scale, but go all the way down to scale degree 6:

1   7   6   5   4   3   2   1   7   6

__ __ __ __ __ __ __ __ __ __

Now, starting on scale degree 6, sing up 8 notes:

6   7   1   2   3   4   5   6

__ __ __ __ __ __ __ __

This is the ____ minor scale.

4. Sing an E♭ major scale:

1	2	3	4	5	6	7	1
E♭	F	__	__	__	__	__	__

Now sing down the scale, but go all the way down to scale degree 6:

1   7   6   5   4   3   2   1   7   6

__ __ __ __ __ __ __ __ __ __

Now, starting on scale degree 6, sing up 8 notes:

6   7   1   2   3   4   5   6

__ __ __ __ __ __ __ __

This is the ____ minor scale.

B. Identify the relative minor of each of the following major keys:

1. G major _____
2. D major _____
3. F major _____
4. B♭ Major _____
5. A Major _____

Identify the relative major of each of the following minor keys (use minor scale pattern of whole and half steps to find scale degree 3):

1. A minor _____
2. B minor _____
3. D minor _____
4. G minor _____
5. F♯ minor _____

PARALLEL MINOR

The **parallel minor** is simply the minor scale that begins on the same pitch. The parallel minor of C major is C minor; the parallel minor of E major is E minor, etc.

RESTORING THE LEADING TONE: *Not really "accidental"*

Since accidentals (see Unit Four) occur frequently in minor keys, let's review them. One of the most comfortable aspects of singing in major keys is the way certain scale degrees have very decisive feelings and pulls. Scale degree 1 always has a sense of finality and solidity; scale degree 7, the leading tone, emphatically leads us back to scale degree 1 almost every time. This helps to anchor the music and gives it structure. So what do we do in minor keys, where the leading tone is not present to plant us firmly back on 1?

When we are in a minor key but still want that strong "7-1" pull at a certain spot, we simply restore it by raising the seventh scale degree to make it a leading tone.

As we learned in Unit Four, when a pitch change occurs that is not in the key signature, we specify the change with an accidental before the affected note.

We often use these pitch changes in minor keys when we want to restore the sense of a leading tone. Note, however, that they will still be treated as accidentals and need to be written in whenever they occur.

REVIEW: *The Natural*

Remember that the natural sign (♮) cancels out any previously noted sharp (♯) or flat (♭) within a measure, whether it has been noted as an accidental or by the key signature.

This is a C minor scale, without the key signature:

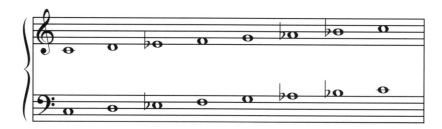

Here is the same C minor scale, with key signature.

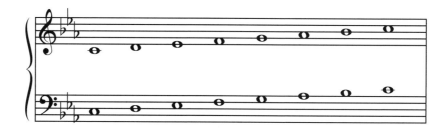

Here is the same minor scale, only this time we've raised the seventh degree. Notice that this time we must specify a B♮ for the seventh degree, since the key signature already contains B♭.

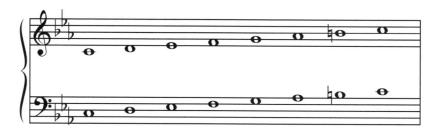

Within any minor key, the raised seventh degree will show up as an accidental, in order for it to cancel out of the key signature.

REVIEW: *Vocabulary*

Accidental: Any note added to a melody that is a change from the noted key signature

Minor: The scale constructed by singing from scale degree 6 up to 6 in any major key. The minor scale matches the key signature of its relative major key, with no accidentals.

Parallel minor/parallel major: The major and minor keys that start on the same pitch but do not share a common key signature

Quality: Designates whether a scale is major or minor

Relative minor/relative major: The major and minor keys that share a common key signature. Each major key has one relative minor key; each minor key has one relative major key.

Singing Melodies in Minor Keys

The procedure for singing a melody in a minor key (or any melody containing accidentals) is nearly the same as for a major key. Follow the same first three steps:

1. Identify the key of the piece. First look at the key signature, which in this melody is one flat. We know that this is the key signature for F major, or its relative minor, D minor. To decide whether the piece is major or minor, there is no definitive answer; you must use clues.

2. What is the starting note? What is the ending note? If the piece starts and ends on F, it is probably in F major. If the piece starts and ends on D, it is probably in D minor. If it starts on F and ends on D, it's probably still in D minor.

3. Do any accidentals occur frequently? Look specifically for the leading tone of whatever the minor key we might be. The leading tone of D minor would be C♯. Do you see any C♯'s in this melody?

Using these two very useful clues, we can decide that the melody is most likely in D minor.

4. Identify the location of the keynote, or first scale degree, on the staff. Circle all occurrences of the pitch D.

5. Assign scale degree numbers to the notated pitches.

UNIT SIX, Page 80

6. Check the melody for any accidentals. Decide whether the accidental will raise or lower the pitch you would normally expect to sing. Indicate which by an arrow pointing either up or down.

7. Now we can sing the melody, altering pitches where necessary to sing the accidentals correctly.

1 2 3 2 3 4 5   4 5 6 7 1 6 5   4 3 2 ♯7 1   1

Just for fun, sing the melody again, without the added C♯ accidental:

1 2 3 2 3 4 5   4 5 6 7 1 6 5   4 3 2 7 1   1

Can you hear how the raised seventh degree, or leading tone, creates a very different sound from the lowered natural seventh degree?

UNIT SIX, Page 81

MELODIC AND RHYTHMIC STUDIES:
Reading Melodies in Minor Keys, in Simple and Compound Meter

Putting It All Together

As always, follow all the steps!

First, identify the time signature, then read the rhythm of the melody, first clapping against the best "background pattern" you can decide on, and then speaking on the syllable *ta*.

Second, using the steps established in Unit Four, practice reading the following melodies by scale degree number only.

Third (and *only* after completing the first two!), read the melody on scale degree numbers in the correct rhythm, or if it is easier, on the syllable *ta*.

1.

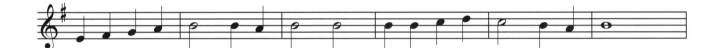

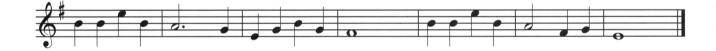

2.

3.

UNIT SIX, Page 83

UNIT SEVEN

Rhythmic Studies:
Finishing Touches — Pickups and Triplets
Melodic and Rhythmic Studies:
Reading Melodies and Rhythms in Simple and Compound Meter, in Major and Minor Keys

At this point, we have learned all the basic building blocks for reading and singing rhythms. All you need to do from here on out is practice! There are just a few more exceptions to the fundamental rules you already know. Two of these in particular are likely to appear in choral music and hymnals: the "pickup measure" or "upbeat," and the "triplet."

RHYTHMIC STUDIES: *Pickups*

Sometimes the first measure of a piece doesn't seem to have enough beats for the time signature. In that case the melody begins with **pickup beats**. It's just a form of musical shorthand indicating that the melody begins in the middle of the measure. Space is not wasted by filling the beginning of the measure with unnecessary rests.

Until you are comfortable enough to take them as they come, the easiest way to deal with pickup measures is to remove the shorthand and count all the rests to determine the beat on which the melody begins. Remember to check the time signature!

Let's look at an example:

According to the time signature, there should be four beats in each measure. But the first measure contains only two eighth notes, which only count for one beat in 4/4 time. This is a typical example of a pickup measure.

UNIT SEVEN, Page 85

While we're learning to count a song with a pickup, just fill in the measure with rests before the pickup notes to make up the correct number of beats for the time signature. In this example, the 4/4 signature indicates four beats per measure, with the quarter note getting one beat.

So if the two eighth notes at the end of the empty bar equal one full beat, we would need to add three beats of rest before those eighth notes to get the correct number of beats. We can notate this in two ways:

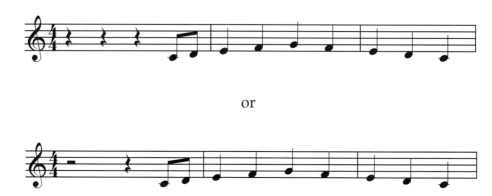

or

To count this melody, then, we'd pick our background pattern—one-and-two-and-three-and-four-and (since eighth notes are present)—and start at the beginning of the measure the way we would in any piece of music:

1 & 2 & 3 & 4 &   1 & 2 & 3 & 4 & ...

With the rests written in, we can see that the pickup in this piece begins on beat 4. Once we've determined this, we can remove the rests and just begin counting and singing on beat 4:

So what happens to the "unused" beats before a pickup? Notice that at the end of the example, there is an incomplete measure as well. If you add the beats from the opening pickup measure to the incomplete final measure, they will add up to a full four-beat measure.

RHYTHMIC STUDIES: *The Triplet*

Most beats in simple meter are only divided in half, but occasionally we want to divide a single beat into three. Rather than altering the time signature, we do this with a **triplet**. A triplet places three notes of equal length within a space of time that would normally require only two of the same kind of note.

Counting triplets

An easy way to speak the count of a triplet is simply to substitute the word "trip-o-let" against your regular background pattern:

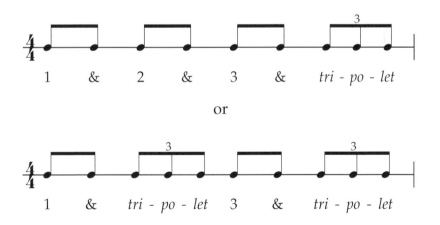

Triplets do not occur very often, but when they do, it's primarily a matter of shifting your thinking for a beat or two, and then immediately returning to the pattern you have set for the rest of the piece.

MELODIC AND RHYTHMIC STUDIES: *Reading Melodies and Rhythms in Simple and Compound Meter, in Major and Minor Keys*

We now have most of the tools needed to read almost any melody we will encounter in our travels. So now let's look at a series of different melodies utilizing the different skills we've learned.

Remember, even though we've learned a great deal, it is still very important to follow all the steps we've practiced, even if it seems we've picked up an awful lot of them! For each of the following exercises, make sure you go through all the steps before attempting to sing the melody as a whole.

Questions to answer before singing a melody

Rhythm: What is the time signature?

1. Is it simple meter or compound meter?
2. What is the smallest note value? What background counting pattern will I need?
3. Have I figured out (written in) how the printed rhythm fits with the background rhythm?
4. What is the beginning beat? Are there any pickup notes?
5. Can I clap the rhythm while speaking the background rhythm?
   Can I speak the rhythm on *ta* while clapping the background rhythm?

Melody: What is the key signature? How many sharps or flats are there?

1. What major key is that time signature?
2. What minor key is that time signature?
3. Which of the two keys—major or minor—is the piece written in?

   a. What are the starting and ending notes? Are they consistent with either the major or minor key of that key signature?

   b. If that didn't give us a conclusive answer, are there any accidentals that occur repeatedly in the examples? Do they match with what would be the raised seventh degree—the leading tone—of the minor key with this key signature?

4. Have I written in the scale degree numbers throughout the melody?
   Have I indicated where any of the accidentals might fall?
5. Can I sing the melody on scale degree numbers?
   Can I sing it on *ta* just thinking the numbers?

Both: Can I then sing the melody through on *ta* in the correct rhythm?

MELODIES TO SING:

For each of the following, go through *all* the steps on page 88 and (only then) sing each melody:

Some of these melodies, as others earlier in the book, are found in your hymnal. So pick up any hymnal and try this yourself!

UNIT EIGHT

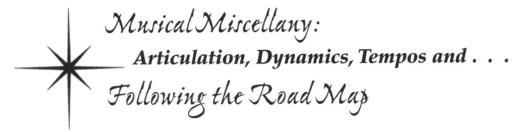

Musical Miscellany:
Articulation, Dynamics, Tempos and . . .
Following the Road Map

So now you've learned pretty much all you need to know to pick up and learn any melody on your own without having to hear it first. However, there are a few more markings, words, and instructions that it will be helpful for you to know. Most of this vocabulary comes from the world of classical music, which still uses the Italian terms.

ARTICULATION: *How are the notes sung?*

Legato (slur): The melody is sung smoothly and evenly, connecting the notes with no space between them; indicated with a smooth curved line connecting the notes.

Staccato: Short crisp notes, separated and unconnected. Indicated by dots directly over or under the notes. (Note that the placement of the dot is different from "dotted notes," which change the note's value. Those dots are placed to the right of the notes, while staccato dots are placed directly over or under the notes.)

Tenuto: Notes are sung with a slight stress or pull on each one, indicated by a small horizontal line over or under the note.

Accent: Indicates that a note should be sung with extra emphasis or stress; indicated by a small horizontal "v" shape over or under the note.

Fermata: Indicates that a note should be held out longer than its printed value; the fermata usually occurs at the end of a piece of music.

DYNAMICS: *How loud or soft are the notes sung?*

Forte: Loud   *f*

Piano: Soft   *p*

Mezzo-forte: Medium loud   *mf*

Mezzo-piano: Medium soft   *mp*

Fortissimo: Very loud   *ff*

Pianissimo: Very soft   *pp*

Crescendo: Becoming louder

Diminuendo: Becoming softer

TEMPO: *How fast are the notes sung?*

Accelerando: Becoming faster

Adagio: Slowly

Allegretto: Rather quickly

Allegro: Quickly

Andante: Medium tempo, neither fast nor slow; "walking" speed

Largo: Extremely slowly

Lento: Very slowly

Moderato: Moderate tempo, faster than Andante, slower than Allegro

Prestissimo: As fast as possible

Presto: Very fast

Rallentando: Slowing down

Ritard or **Ritardando:** Becoming slower

Vivace: Lively

FOLLOW THE ROAD MAP: *Repeats, Endings, and Other Directions*

In contemporary music involving refrains and verses, composers and publishers will often shorten a musical score by using repeats and other directions to avoid printing out pages and pages of identical music. Let's look at the most common shortcuts:

Repeat sign:

    A repeat sign looks like this:

One repeat sign, as in the example on page 93, means to repeat from the beginning of the piece. If a shorter repeat is desired, repeat signs are placed at either end of the passage to be repeated, as below:

Sometimes we want to repeat most of a section of music, but the last measure or two will be different the first and second time. In this case we use first and second "endings":

In the example above, we sing the first two measures, followed by the measure marked "1" (or "first ending"). At the end of that measure, we see a repeat sign, which means we go back to the beginning and take the repeat. But this time after we sing the first two measures, we skip the measure marked "1" and go directly to the "second ending," the measure marked "2."

This can go on indefinitely, if you need to repeat the first section more than once:

In the example above, you start at the beginning, sing the first two measures, sing ending "1," then repeat back to the beginning; sing the first two measures, sing ending "2" (same as ending 1) , repeat back to the beginning; sing the first two measures, and then go to the "third" ending. Always look carefully at the numbers of the endings; they will tell you where to go and when to go there.

 **Note:** Just like the processes we go through to read notes and rhythms, these directions are something to figure out before you actually try to sing a piece of music. Always scan through a piece before you sing so you know where you're going!

Da Capo, Dal Segno, Al Fine, Al Coda, and other confusing Italian instructions

Actually, they are not all that confusing once you become accustomed to them. These are more detailed instructions that indicate exactly where to jump in on a piece of music—again, primarily to save paper and space.

Al coda: Until you reach the ⊕ symbol; then skip to the coda section at the end

Al fine: Until you reach the "fine"

Coda: (Italian for "tail") A section added at the end of a piece of music that basically gives a good conclusion to the piece and is probably somewhat different from what has come before; indicated by the symbol ⊕

D. C. or Da Capo: Go back and start again from the beginning (*capo* means "head")

D. S. or Dal Segno: Go back and start again from the "sign." In music, the sign is 𝄋; go back to the point in the piece where you see the 𝄋 and sing again from there.

Fine: (pronounced FEE-nay) The end of the piece. If the road map causes the piece to end somewhere in what looks like the middle of the page, the word "fine" will often indicate this.

Let's use a familiar hymn tune to illustrate some of these different possibilities. (A hymn this short would almost never be abbreviated like this; we're doing this now merely to illustrate these examples.)

Here is the hymn tune HYMN TO JOY ("Joyful, Joyful, We Adore You") written the way you would normally see it:

Now suppose we wanted to shorten it, using the "D. S. al Fine" directions. It would look like this:

Follow the road map:

Start at the beginning (making a mental note of the 𝄋 and "Fine" markings on the way; we don't need to do anything about them until the second time around) and sing until the end, where we see "D. S. al Fine." Then jump back to the 𝄋 and sing the final four measures until the word "Fine." This tells us that we're at the end, so we stop. This road map, using only twelve measures of printed music, gives us the exact same piece of music as the original sixteen-measure version.

Let's look at another way to write the same hymn, this one a little more intricate.

Here we've gotten the original sixteen measures down to a mere nine on the printed page. Let's look at the road map of this version and see what we get.

We start at the beginning and sing until our first road map clue:

This tells us to go back and repeat from the beginning. Next time around, since the ending is marked only "1," we will skip that measure.

This time around, we skip the first ending and jump directly to the second ending. As before, we see the word "Fine," but all we have to do for now is notice that it's there; nothing has told us to do anything about it yet. We also notice that this ending has a "3" in it as well. There's no repeat sign or anything of the kind in this measure, so we don't need to worry about it yet, but this is a signal to us that we will see this measure again.

After singing the first phrase with first and second endings, we go on to the next section:

As we expected earlier when we saw the word "Fine," here we come to our directions telling us what to do with it. We are told, "D. C. al Fine," or "Da capo—back to the top—and sing until the word 'Fine' appears." So we do:

UNIT EIGHT, Page 97

Lo and behold, here is our opportunity to sing the third ending. We sing the first three measures, skip the first ending (since we've already sung it), and go to the third ending, where now we know to end the piece at the word "Fine."

This is far more confusing than a sixteen-measure hymn tune ever needs to be, and we've only gone through this exercise to illustrate how some of this works. In longer pieces these repeats and road maps can save reams of paper—not to mention time, since choral singers will only have to mark their parts on a refrain once instead of having to transfer markings to what is essentially the same page three or four times in a single choral piece.

We will close this chapter with an examination of some actual choral pieces, looking at how dynamics, articulation, and other musical information work together with printed notes and rhythms to make a complete musical setting.

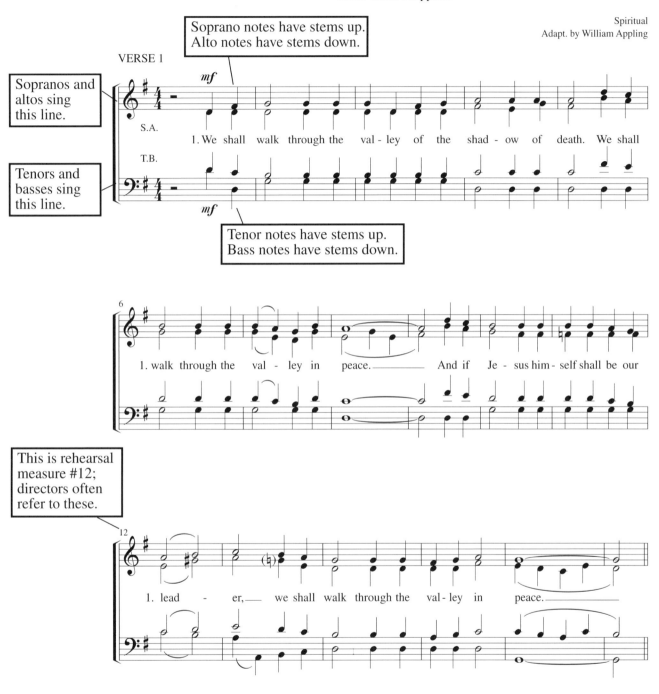

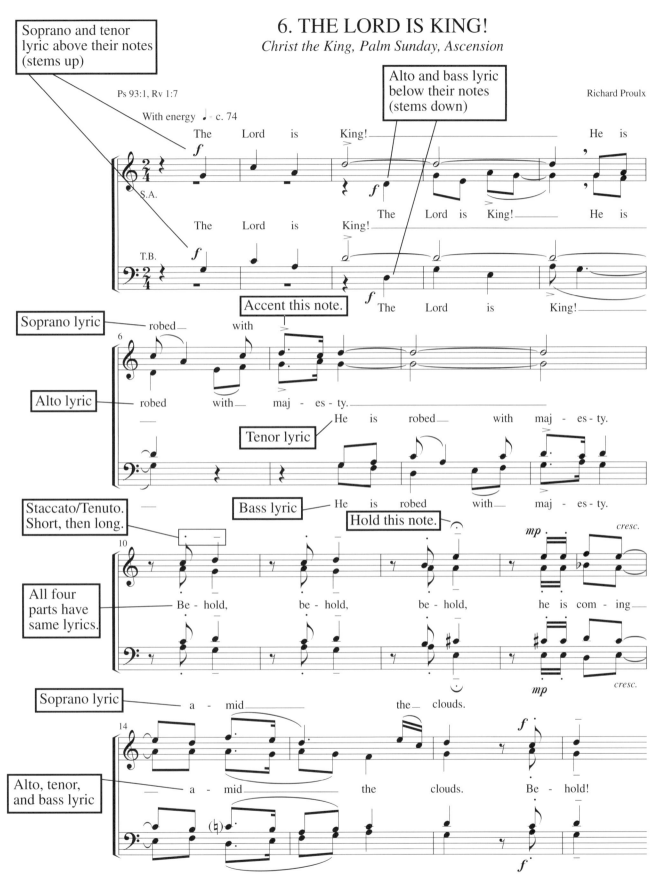

APPENDIX A

The Major Scales and Their Key Signatures

C major

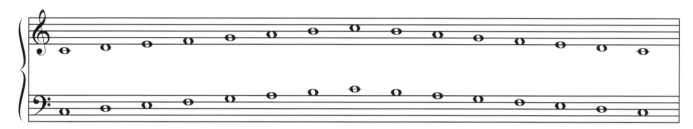

F major

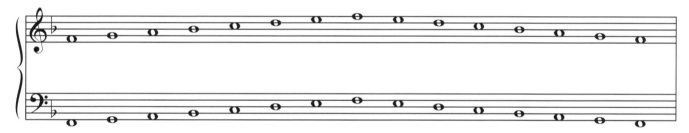

B♭ major

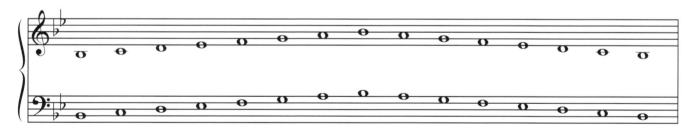

APPENDIX A, Page 105

E♭ major

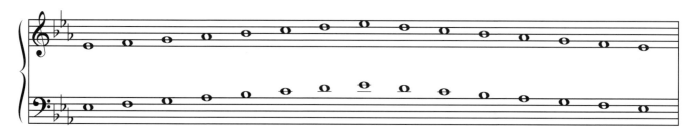

A♭ major

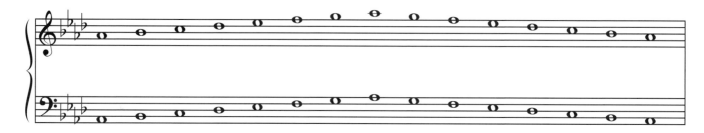

D♭ major

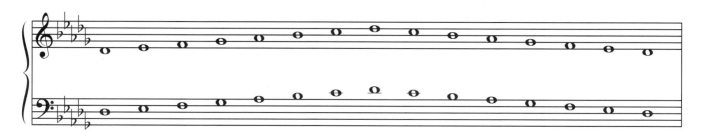

G♭ major

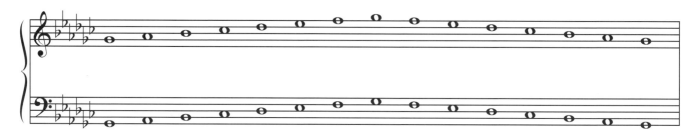

G major

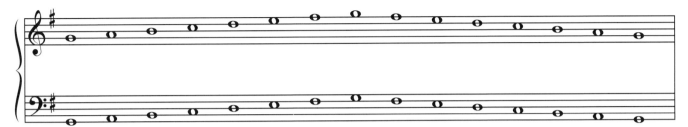

D major

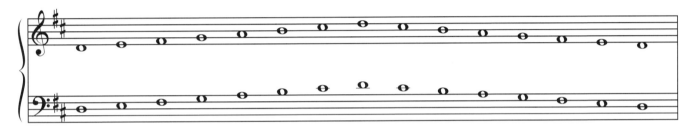

A major

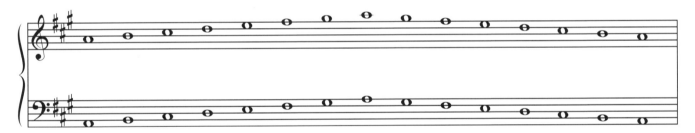

E major

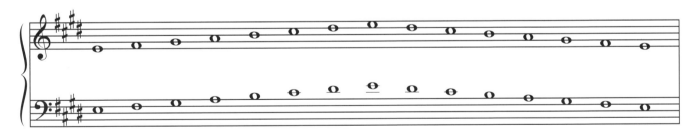

B major

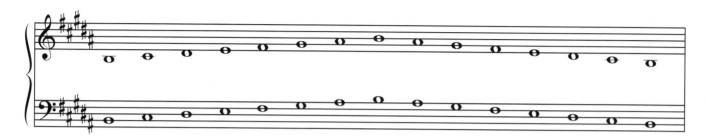

F# major

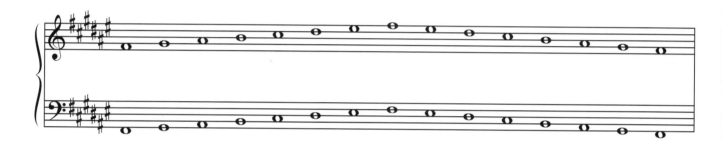

APPENDIX A, Page 108

APPENDIX B

The Natural Minor Scales and Their Key Signatures

A minor

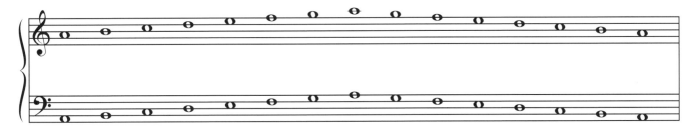

D minor

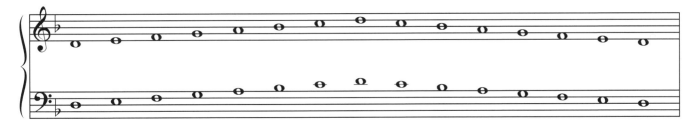

G minor

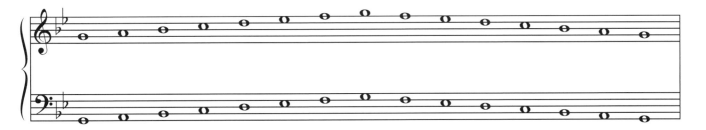

C minor

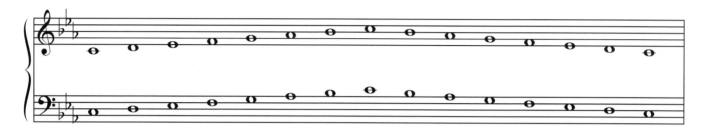

F minor

B♭ minor

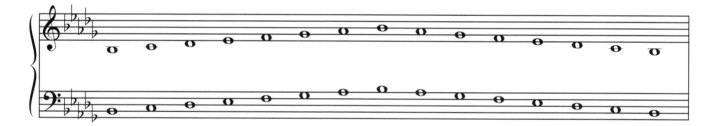

E♭ minor

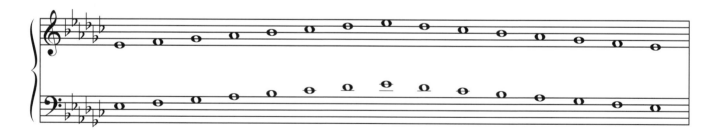

E minor

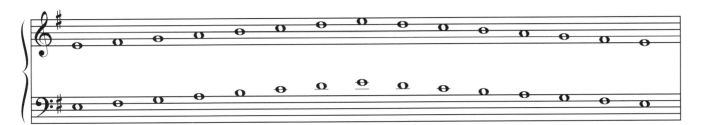

B minor

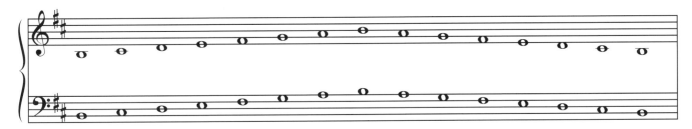

F# minor

C# minor

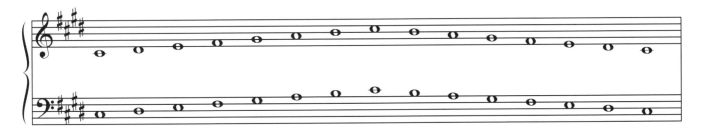

G♯ minor

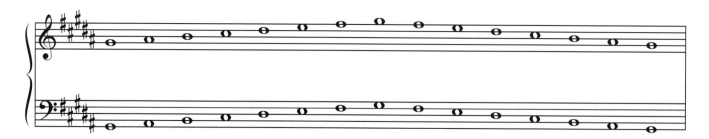

 Note: Music is rarely written in G♯ minor, and almost never in D♯ minor. Usually their **enharmonic** keys—A♭ minor/E♭ minor—are used.

APPENDIX C

The Bass Clef and Treble Clef Staff

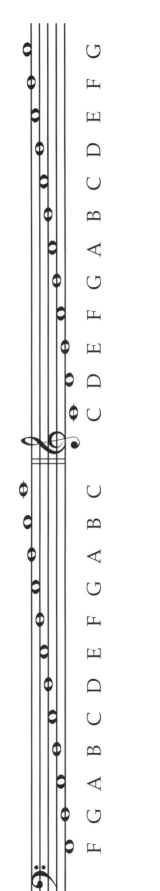

The Piano Keyboard:

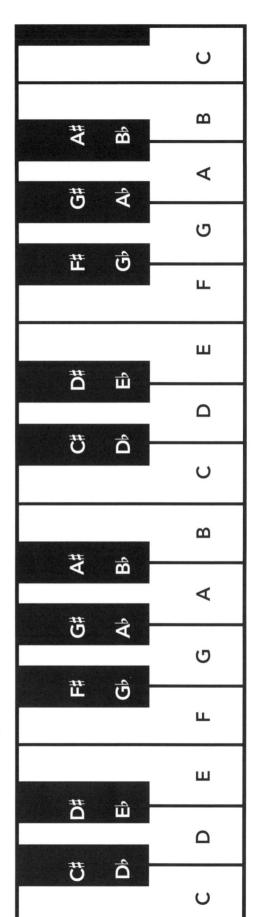

APPENDIX C, Page 113